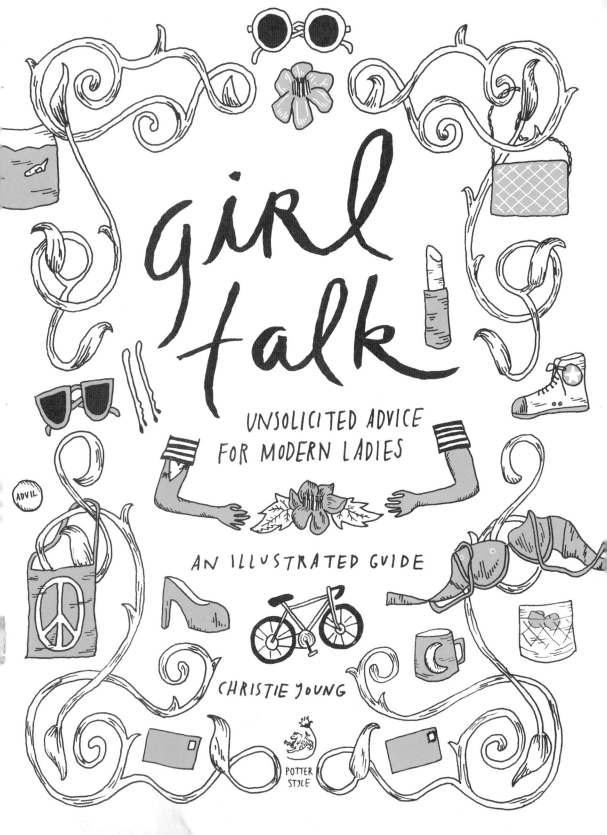

girl talk

UNSOLICITED ADVICE FOR MODERN LADIES

AN ILLUSTRATED GUIDE

CHRISTIE YOUNG

POTTER STYLE

Published in the United States by Potter Style, an imprint of
the Crown Publishing Group, a division of Random House LLC,
a Penguin Random House Company, New York.
www.crownpublishing.com   www.clarksonpotter.com

POTTER STYLE is a trademark and POTTER with colophon
is a registered trademark of Random House LLC.

Library of Congress Cataloging-in-Publication Data is
available upon request.

ISBN 978-0-385-34554-5
eBook ISBN 978-0-385-34558-3
Printed in China

Book design by Christie Young
Cover and interior illustrations by Christie Young
Cover design by Danielle Deschenes & Christie Young

10 9 8 7 6 5 4 3 2 1
First Edition

Girl Talk is the ladies' room of conversation. It's fine if people listen, but consider it sacred. It's a safe house for your insecure side & a private party for period woes. It's a place where good friends are made & bad friends have hexes put on them (because they deserve it) & there are no time limits because that door is always open. It's a place where details make all the difference & you better go for gory or go home because otherwise what's the point?

Think of this book as that place, or if you're down on your luck, as a friend. You might need advice or you might just need to chill with a like-minded lady. In this book, anything goes. Bodies, boys, boys' bodies, friends, families—let's talk about it. It's not always paradise outside those doors, but cross my heart & hope to die, you're gonna be totally fine.

It's safe to say that if you grew up anywhere that isn't New York (or Paris, for the orphan/Madeline fans), you've spent some time dreaming of "getting out of this place." The small-mindedness! The heat! The Cracker Barrels! Ahhh! And then you are old enough to leave but young enough to use your top 3 MASH destinations as a guide, and you go there and find out it's freaky as fuck because where are your friends? And my God, Cracker Barrel exists everywhere. Give it a year, and then give it 5. These things take time.

MAKING THE MOVE

Sometimes you move because you want to (grad school!) and other times you move because you have to (protective custody!). Regardless of the reason, making the most of it makes all the difference. Cable is everywhere, but the Alamo is not —so get out there, wherever there may be.

PLAN AHEAD/HAVE ENOUGH:

  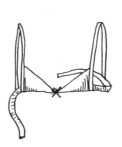 

KNOW BEFORE YOU GO:

 **WHERE:** OLD TOWN / NEW TOWN / FANTASY TOWN / COLLEGE TOWN / RETIREMENT COMMUNITY

WHEN: RIGHT NOW / RIGHT AFTER SCHOOL / RIGHT AFTER A BREAKUP / WHEN IT'S 75° OUT

WHY: YOU NEED A CHANGE / WANT SEASONS / WANT OPTIONS / BIG FISH IN SMALL POND

BE MY NEIGHBOR
JUST DON'T BE MY MOTHER

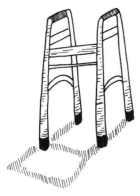

THE ELDERLY

GRANDPARENTS WITHOUT THE GIFTS—
THEY HATE LOUD MUSIC BUT THEY'VE
GOT A LOT OF LOVE TO GIVE. THEY
CARE ABOUT LAWNS & LAWS &
LOOKING THROUGH YOUR WINDOWS.

THE INEPT

5-10 YEARS YOUR JUNIOR WITH NOTHING
BUT BONG RIFFS TO OFFER YOU. THEY
HAVE NO SHAME (& NO LAWN MOWER)
BUT BOY DO THEY HAVE AN ENDLESS
SUPPLY OF 4AM SUBLIME.

THE UNDERSTANDABLE

YOU GIVE A LITTLE, YOU GET A LITTLE—
THEY HAVE LOUD BBQS, YOU HAVE
AN INSATIABLE LOVE FOR GRACELAND.
COUNT ON EACH OTHER FOR BAKING
NEEDS, ADVICE & BARBITUATES.

THE SANTERIA GUY

You'll know him by the dead chickens & candles.

THE CAN COLLECTOR

She rifles through your garbage every M/W/F.

WHO'S WHO ON THE BLOCK (YOUR BLOCK)

the **SHREK**
TOFU CUTLET
AVOCADO
SPINACH &
HUMMUS

THE DELI STAFF

knows what you like when you like it (at a discount!)

THE STUD BARISTA

Gives you a whole new reason to get dressed.

GETTING

METHOD

THERE'S NO NEED TO GET LOST, UNLESS SOMEONE IS TELLING YOU TO. RUN IT, ROLL IT, OR RIDE IT, JUST MAKE SURE YOU LEARN IT (OR HAVE A MAP ON YOU).

WALK: Same rules as hiking apply — bring plenty of water, always have a phone on you, and make a lot of noise/motion if in danger (aka run).

BUS: The cheapest & easiest way to get from the Hasidic to the Haitian neighborhood. Comes with free A/C, but best done in daylight & while sober.

BIKE: Sweatiest of all options, but the fastest way to get around (and to get away). Always wear a helmet, never wear heels.

AROUND

WATCH YOUR BACK

LIVING IN A NEW PLACE CAN BE SCARY—GETTING LOST & MUGGED IS EVEN SCARIER. LEARN YOUR TURF & YOU'LL NEVER BE CAUGHT OFF GUARD BY CRIMINALS.

Count the dime bags on your walk to work—the route with the most empties wins!

LAW & ORDER

How many episodes take place on your block?

Learn to differentiate thunder, gun shots & fireworks with your eyes closed!

STOLEN!

LAST SEEN LOCKED UP. PLEASE CALL!

Does everything seem to be missing? Leave nothing outdoors.

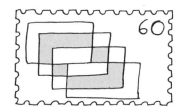

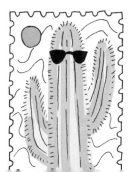

Keep In Touch...

YOU'RE IN A NEW PLACE-NOW WHAT? SEND SOME REAL MAIL! REMIND PEOPLE THAT YOU'VE MOVED, LET SOMEONE KNOW HOW MUCH YOU LOVE CARE PACKAGES, OR JUST SEND A LETTER TO YOURSELF BECAUSE YOU NEED A REASON TO GO OUTSIDE.

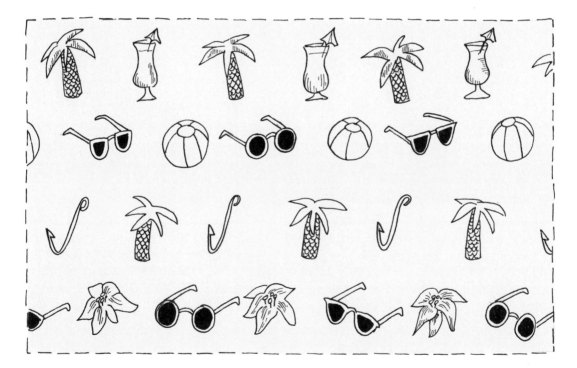

REMEMBER! POSTAGE IS LESS FOR POSTCARDS THAN REGULAR MAIL.

WRITER'S BLOCK?

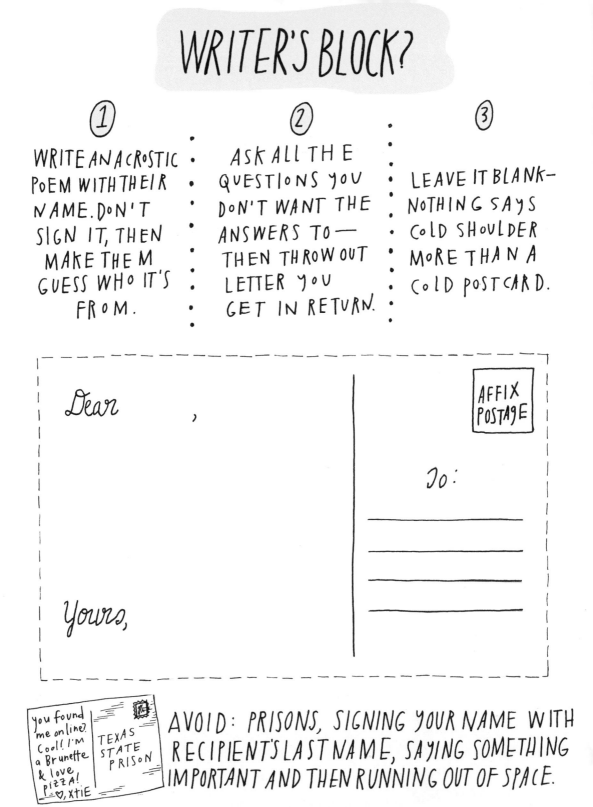

① WRITE AN ACROSTIC POEM WITH THEIR NAME. DON'T SIGN IT, THEN MAKE THEM GUESS WHO IT'S FROM.

② ASK ALL THE QUESTIONS YOU DON'T WANT THE ANSWERS TO — THEN THROW OUT LETTER YOU GET IN RETURN.

③ LEAVE IT BLANK— NOTHING SAYS COLD SHOULDER MORE THAN A COLD POSTCARD.

Dear   ,

Yours,

AFFIX POSTAGE

To:

you found me online? Cool! I'M a Brunette & love PIZZA! ♡, XTIE

TEXAS STATE PRISON

AVOID: PRISONS, SIGNING YOUR NAME WITH RECIPIENT'S LAST NAME, SAYING SOMETHING IMPORTANT AND THEN RUNNING OUT OF SPACE.

GET OUT THERE

YOU FORGET HOW MUCH A PLACE HAS TO OFFER UNTIL YOU'RE FORCED TO GO OUTSIDE BECAUSE YOUR A/C IS BROKEN & YOU NEED MORE POPSICLES. ALL YOU REALLY NEED IS A BOOK, A BLANKET & A SNACK & YOU'LL BE SITTING PRETTY FOR PEOPLE-WATCHING.

THE PARK

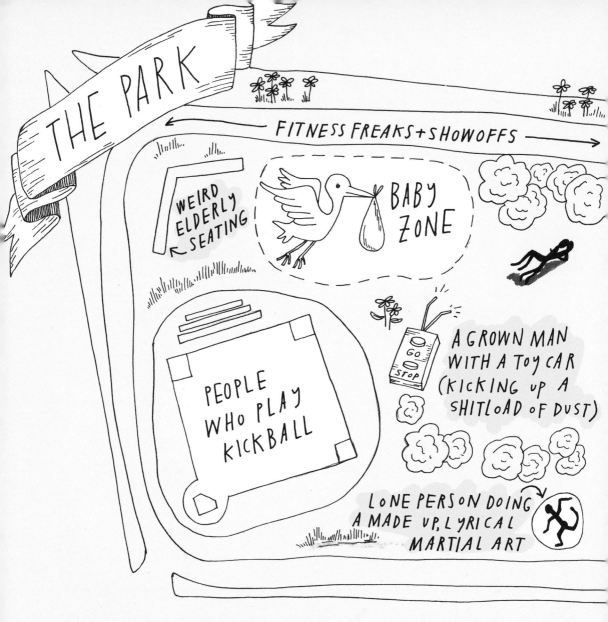

FITNESS FREAKS + SHOWOFFS

WEIRD ELDERLY SEATING

BABY ZONE

A GROWN MAN WITH A TOY CAR (KICKING UP A SHITLOAD OF DUST)

GO
STOP

PEOPLE WHO PLAY KICKBALL

LONE PERSON DOING A MADE UP, LYRICAL MARTIAL ART

PACK BEFORE YOU PARK IT — YOU DON'T WANT

WATER

Topo

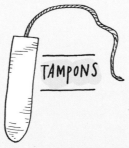

TAMPONS

SWEATER THAT DOUBLES AS A PILLOW

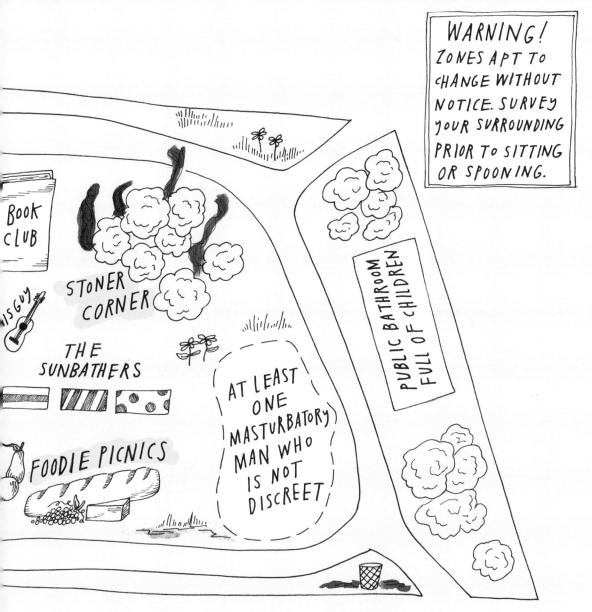

WARNING! ZONES APT TO CHANGE WITHOUT NOTICE. SURVEY YOUR SURROUNDING PRIOR TO SITTING OR SPOONING.

BOOK CLUB

'IS GUY

STONER CORNER

THE SUNBATHERS

FOODIE PICNICS

AT LEAST ONE MASTURBATORY MAN WHO IS NOT DISCREET

PUBLIC BATHROOM FULL OF CHILDREN

TO LEAVE UNTIL YOU'RE READY

MY SNACKS

SUNSCREEN

LADIES CHOICE! WILL IT BE A TRASHY BOOK OR A WALLET OF WEED? YOU DECIDE!

the RECORD STORE

FINDING A RECORD STORE YOU LIKE DOESN'T HAVE TO BE STRESSFUL. SOME PEOPLE LIKE SHOPPING AROUND — THIS PERSON LIKES KNOWING THERE'S ONE PLACE TO GO WITH ATTRACTIVE EMPLOYEES & FAIR PRICES.

AT FIRST YOU MIGHT BE TEMPTED TO STAY IN & LOOK ON iTUNES — I'M NOT HERE TO JUDGE, BUT YOU'RE NOT GOING TO GET ANY FRESH AIR OR MEET SOMEONE THAT WAY — SO GO EXPLORE!

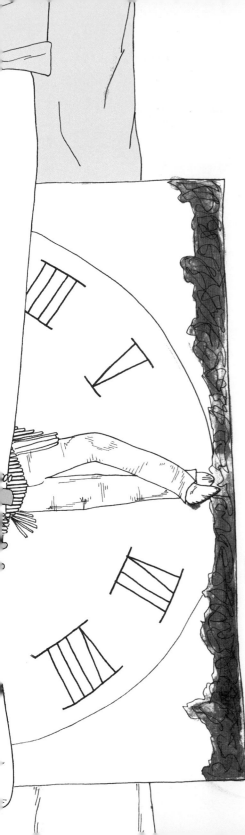

THE CHECKLIST:

☐ Employees who will talk to you but not talk too much or too loudly or too snobby.

☐ There is some high-quality stuff but also some low-quality, $1 bins in case you like that kind of thing.

☐ The customers are equal parts stoners/loners/DJs/dad-types.

☐ There are places to hide in case you're fighting with your roommate and/or you want to act out Where the Heart Is (minus the baby).

☐ Lice-free headphones at the listening station unless you are 10 and currently have them.

Coffee Shopping

YOU CAN SAVE A BUNCH OF MONEY & MAKE COFFEE AT HOME OR YOU CAN SPEND $3/DAY FOR A YEAR UNTIL YOU START GETTING YOUR ICED RED EYES FOR FREE. SOME PREFER THE LATTER, SERVED UP BY A MUSCLED MAN WITH A NECK TATTOO. CHOOSE CAREFULLY, ESPECIALLY IF YOU'RE ADDICTED.

THE PLACES YOU'LL GO:

- STUDY HALL SHOP   • DOUBLES AS VEGAN BAKERY
- OVERPRICED ESPRESSO SHOP   • PACKED WITH STROLLERS
- EMPLOYED WITH BARISTAS YOU WANT TO BANG (SEE ABOVE
- THE FRENCH PASTRY PLACE • THE SHOP WITH BOTTOMLESS CUPS

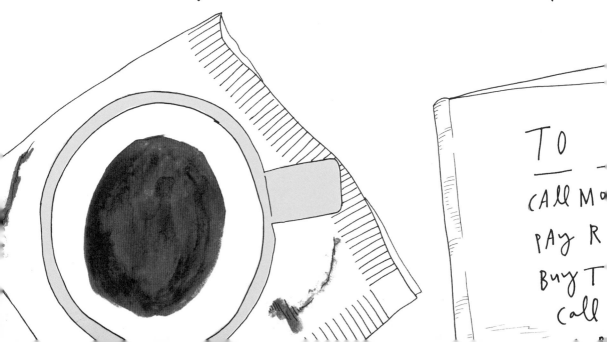

TO

CALL Mo
PAY R
BUY T
CALL

THE PEOPLE YOU'LL SEE:

- PEOPLE WHO PAY IN CHANGE   • PATCHOULI PEOPLE
- GIRLS ON PERMANENT DIETS • DUDES WHO TALK PHILOSOPHY
- UNEMPLOYED BLOGGERS   • BOOK SNOBS • GENERAL SNOBS
- WELL-DRESSED FREELANCERS (WHERE DO THEY COME FROM?!)

THE QUALITY OF THE CUP:

SHITTY BUT CHEAP   • SHITTY BUT ON WAY TO WORK
EXPENSIVE BUT SO GOOD & GIRL YOU DESERVE IT
AN A+ CUP BUT HAS A STUPID NAME LIKE "SEXY BABY CUP"
BETTER THAN McDONALD'S   • WORSE THAN DUNKIN' DONUTS

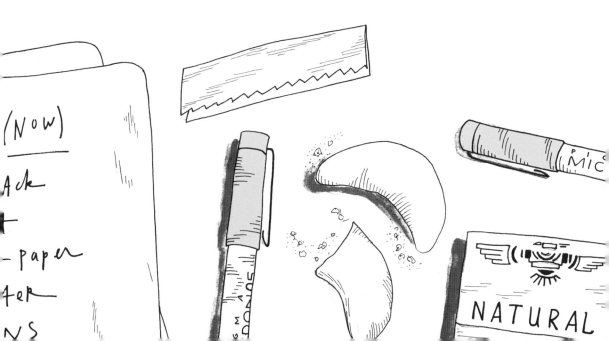

The BEACH

SUMMER IS HOT, SWEATING IS NOT. FORGET YOUR FLAWS & PAY RESPECT TO THE WATER GODS — IT'S YOUR ONLY HOPE OF SURVIVING THE SUMMER.

BRING A TOWEL YOU CAN RECOGNIZE/ NO ONE WILL MISTAKE FOR THEIRS

READING MATERIAL

CLOTHES YOU CAN PUT ON WHEN WET/STICKY/ DEHYDRATED

A BAG NO ONE WILL WANT TO STEAL

SNACKS & BEERS & WATER (AD INFINITUM)

PLENTY OF SUNSCREEN

CHOOSE YOUR BEACH COMPANY CAREFULLY — NOTHING BUT GOOD VIBES (/VIBRATIONS) BELONG AT THE BEACH.

WORST-CASE
True Stories

YOU'RE SUNBATHING AND FEEL SOMETHING
FALL ON YOUR BACK & REALIZE IT'S A HAM
SANDWICH THAT FELL OUT OF A SEAGULL'S MOUTH
& HE'S COMING BACK FOR THE REST.

YOU GET TOO EXCITED ABOUT JUMPING
INTO THE WAVES & DON'T REALIZE YOU ARE
BOTH SUNNING & MOONING EVERYONE ON YOUR
WAY OUT OF THE WATER (THANKS, BOTTOMS!).

NOTICING YOUR FORGOTTEN BIKINI LINE
MINUTES BEFORE NOTICING YOUR EXBF 2 TOWELS DOWN.

BEST-CASE
Possibilities

YOU FIND A BABY-FREE & BUG-FREE BEACH.

YOU LEAVE BEACH WITHOUT ANY SAND STILL IN BUTT / CROTCH / BACKPACK / SHOES.

IT TURNS OUT YOUR PERFECT BEACH HAIR IS PERMANENT, NOW AND FOREVER.

NOT A SINGLE HAIR WAS MISSED WHEN SHAVING AND YOU HAVE NO SUNBURN TO SPEAK OF AND SOMEONE BROUGHT SO MANY SNACKS & IT WASN'T THE SEAGULL.

EVERY FESTIVAL REQUIRES 2 THINGS: A TICKET & A PLAN.
ASIDE FROM THAT YOUR BAG IS YOUR OYSTER—PACK
IT FULL OF TREASURE & YOU WON'T BE DISAPPOINTED.
BRING TOILETRIES IF YOU DON'T PLAN ON GOING
HOME, OTHERWISE YOU CAN PLAN ON GETTING NASTY.

MUSIC FESTIVALS

- Not for the faint of heart, unless you know where the medical tent is (it's gonna be far).

- Front row / backstage / onstage rules, but don't get kicked out for wanting to "touch them."

- You will look beautiful by the end of it! Just kidding, you'll look like a meth-head if it's outdoors.

BOOK FESTIVALS

- So much free swag but you'll also spend a butt-load even though everything's on Amazon.

- A great way to meet people while also a great way to ensure you'll stay in to read.

- Dress to impress because Peter Sagal might be there & he's wearing a suit.

ANIMAL FUNCTIONS

- Plan on petting every animal there — do not plan on eating the nachos they're selling unless you have gloves.

- Build extra time into your schedule in case there's an animal fashion show.   Never say no to cat couture.

- Only bring $20 with you — it's not enough to adopt an animal, and if it is, tell yourself you want dinner more.

· ·

COMIC CON

- Will it be full of pleasure or pain? Don't go unless you can answer this for sure.

- Of all fests, this will be the most crucial for a cell phone & a camera (the kids are cute).

- A real test of strength — both for your theatrical eyeliner and willingness to wait in lines.

REE
MUSIC
THIS WAY

You've moved out of your parents' house. You have 5 roommates. You live alone. You live alone with 5 aloe plants. You prefer dinner parties to paying for cable, and sometimes plants to people. That's fine. It's about feeling presentable in the present company, even when that means just you.

FINDING ROOMIES

The very worst roommates you can find are on Craigslist, but so are the most mediocre of apartments in your price range. It's a freakfest out there, so be careful what you wish for — chances are they'll eat all of your ice cream (& maybe your undies).

ANTONIO

- Eats ½ gallon of ice cream daily
- Parks 18-wheeler in front of house
- Will kill your fish one day (RIP Taco)

SUSAN

- Law-school student (hates "noise")
- Doesn't understand brevity in texts
- Has parents respond to Craigslist ads

ROSALIND

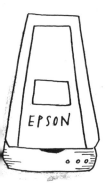

- Sleeps in your bed for a month
- Puts empty beer bottles in fridge (??)
- Will loan you her scanner as payment

SCOTT

- Rents out living room to strangers
- Feeds cats loudly (I mean...)
- Will accuse you of "spilling things" over text

Qualities to look for

 AN EXTENSIVE LE CREUSET COLLECTION

 WEARS A 9½ JUST LIKE YOU!

 why did the pizza cross the Road?

DECENT JOKE TELLER (BUT NOT BETTER THAN YOU)

 BLAH BLAH BLAH BOOOO HOO

IS NEITHER A CHATTY CATHY NOR DEBBIE DOWNER

Testing the potential roommate

 Diary

- LEAVE DIARY OUT
- GO TO BATHROOM
- ASK QUESTIONS ONLY DIARY WOULD KNOW

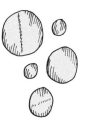

- OFFER DRINKS & DRUGS
- JUDGE THEM ACCORDINGLY

- ASK IF THEY PREFER FLOUR OR CORN TORTILLAS
- THERE'S ONLY ONE RIGHT ANSWER (FLOUR, OBV)

- ROLE-PLAY VARIOUS SCENARIOS WITH 'EM
- SEE HOW WELL THEY DO WITH THE TICKLING ONE

ALL THINGS CONSIDERED

SO YOU WANT TO LIVE ALONE? EXPECT A FEW OF THESE CH-CH-CHANGES.

ROOMIES ⟶ ROOM FOR ONE

SOMEONE ELSE'S DISHES...

EVERY DISH ALONE.

CLOTHES FOR DAYS...

MORE LAUNDRY DAYS.

PARTY ALL THE TIME...

PARTY OF ONE.

SO YOU WANT A ROOMMATE? COMPATIBILITY IS THE KEY.

IF YOU'RE... ⟶ LOOK FOR...

A SLEEPWALKER — SOMEONE WITH LOCK OCD

DIETING — GLUTEN-FREE

ASHANTI — JA RULE

FURNISHING

Once you've cleaned up your space (tiny apartment), it's time to make it a home. All it takes is a little time, a little effort & a medium-sized rug. If home is where the heart is, make sure it's dressed to the nines.

BED: IF YOU'RE BROKE, INVEST IN A GOOD BED FIRST— IF YOU'RE RICH, INVEST IN A TEMPURPEDIC.

COUCH: GET ONE THAT FITS YOU—A LOVE SEAT IS CHILD'S PLAY. ALSO NEVER SUBSTITUTE A COUCH FOR A BED.

LIGHTING: FORGET OVERHEAD LIGHTS, EMBRACE THE LAMP. SUPPLEMENT WITH CANDLES.

DECORATING: THIS IS YOUR TIME TO SHINE! PAINT THE WALLS, HANG SOME POSTERS & ENJOY.

KITCHEN: LINENS ARE VITAL, VINTAGE LINENS ARE A GAME CHANGER & A KITCHENAID = WOMANHOOD.

CURTAINS: FOR BOTH YOUR SAFETY & YOUR SANITY. CAN DOUBLE AS A TOWEL IN A PINCH.

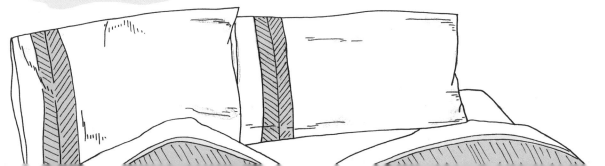

PRACTICE MAKES PERFECT

IT'S NOT ABOUT WHAT YOU HAVE, IT'S WHERE YOU PUT IT. TRY DRAWING WHAT YOU HAVE FIRST, AND WHAT YOU WANT SECOND. YOU CAN'T GO WRONG IF YOU USE A PENCIL.

HOUSE PARTIES

YOU DON'T HAVE TO PARTY HARD TO PARTY WELL. WHETHER IT'S A PARTY OF 5, 50, OR 1 MAKES NO DIFFERENCE, AS LONG AS YOU'RE HAVING A GOOD TIME. THE BEST HOSTESS IS A HAPPY HOSTESS, SO DON'T SWEAT OVER SUPPER OR FREAK OUT OVER FREAK DANCING — IT'S YOUR PARTY & YOUR RULES.

PART ONE
THE INVITE

TEXT

INTERNET

FLYER

TELL NO ONE
(PARTY OF ONE)

PART TWO
REFRESHMENTS

BOOZE
(SOMETHING NICE)

BEER
(SOMETHING CHEAP)

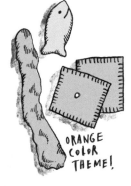

SNAX
(SOMETHING PORTABLE)

PILLS
(ADVIL IS ALWAYS APPRECIATED)

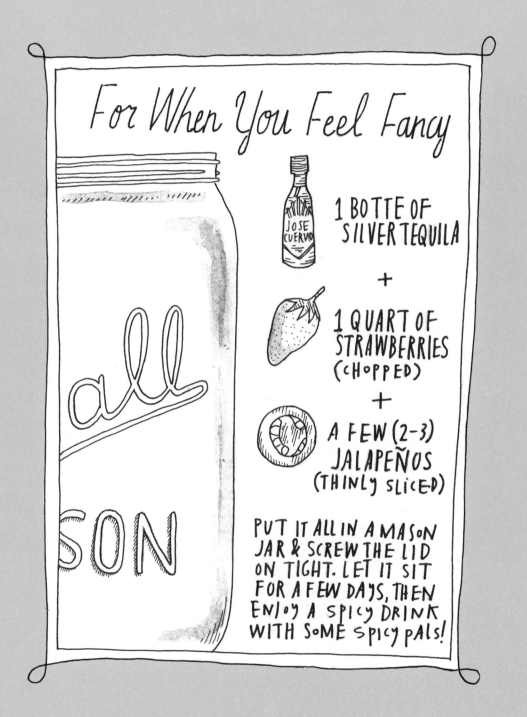

PART THREE
THE PLAYLIST

SADE
SLOW JAMS

TOP 40
DANCE!

RADIO

YOUTUBE
(DANGEROUS)

PART FOUR
ATTIRE

FLASHY

FANCY

FREAKY

(NO SHOES!)
DTF

PART FIVE
PARTY RULES

NEVER PRETEND TO BE ANYTHING YOU'RE NOT—YOU'LL END UP WITH
A PARTY FULL OF IDIOTS OR D-BAGS • LEAVE SNACKS OUT AT NIGHT
TO EAT WHILE CLEANING NEXT DAY • HIDE VALUABLES • HIDE MEDS •
HIDE BOYFRIEND (J/K) • THERE IS NOTHING WRONG WITH CHANGING
CLOTHES OR PUTTING ON PAJAMAS • YOU ARE ALLOWED TO DENY
ENTRY TO ANYONE/EVERYONE • YOU CALL ALL THE SHOTS!

CLEANING

A clean home says lady, an untidy home says loose. And a shower wall covered in hair says lazy with a touch of anemia. Remember, nothing says sexy like getting into bed without dusting dirt off your feet. Especially if you have a guest. Dirty floor = dirty feet = dirty sheets.

THE ALWAYS-CLEAN CHECKLIST

Bedroom

- ☐ LINENS
- ☐ COMFORTER
- ☐ CURTAINS
- ☐ UNDER BED, IF VISIBLE

Bathroom

- ☐ TOILET BOWL
- ☐ TRASH BIN
- ☐ ALL DRAINS
- ☐ TOOTHPASTE ON THE WATER FAUCET

Beyond

- ☐ KITCHEN SINK
- ☐ FRIDGE
- ☐ PANTRY
- ☐ ANYWHERE THERE'S DIRT

TIP: NEVER CLEAN A TOILET WITH TOILET PAPER—STAY FULLY STOCKED WITH THE MOST BASIC OF BASICS.

Sheets

DO NOT WAIT FOR SHEETS TO BECOME VISIBLY DIRTY. IF YOU FLOW IN IT OR BRO IN IT, CHANGE THEM SOONER RATHER THAN LATER.

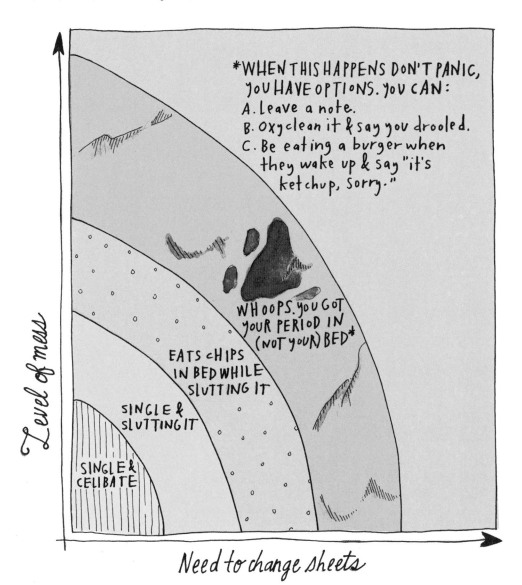

CLEANING FOR YOUR
OVERNIGHT GUESTS

SOMETIMES YOU PLAN FOR OVERNIGHT GUESTS & SOMETIMES YOU HAVE 5 MINUTES TO SHAVE YOUR LEGS BECAUSE SOMEONE IS GOING TO TOUCH THEM. DIFFERENT GUESTS CALL FOR VERY DIFFERENT PREPARATIONS, SO THE BEST THING YOU CAN DO IS BE READY FOR FRIEND, FOE, OR FREAK ALIKE.

Family

My mother cried when she saw my first apartment & my uncle always demands a sandwich. Stock up on snacks, booze (for them & you), clean linens & a clean internet search history.

Friend

The quality of the set-up should correlate to the quality of the friend. Always leave a trash can nearby & if you're feeling generous, a glass of water.

Sexy Friend

Nothing's worse than not getting laid because you ran out of condoms (do **not** run out of self-respect). If sexy is in the stars (yes!), protect yo'self & have fresh sheets.

PESTS

House pests are just that—pests. Even the word "vermin" sounds like something you would catch from a one-night stand who wears cologne & leaves the condom on the floor; just like a dead bug, dried up & on the ground.

HOW TO HANDLE BUGS, PESTS & OTHER GROSS THINGS

1. FIND IT

STEALING YOUR CHIPS

WAITING FOR YOU TO GET HOME AT 3AM

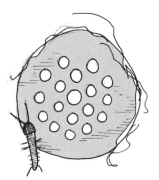

PEEPING ON YOU IN THE SHOWER

2. FIND IT BY ACCIDENT

1. PACK UP APARTMENT BEFORE MOVING. MOVE DRESSER FROM WALL.

2. FIND FAVE SHIRT BEHIND DRESSER. REACH TO TRY IT ON.

3. FIND MOUSE THAT TRIED IT ON & LOVED IT TO DEATH. (SEEMINGLY MONTHS AGO)

3. IDENTIFY IT

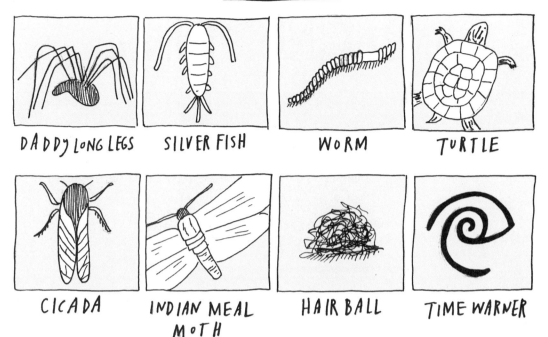

DADDY LONG LEGS   SILVER FISH   WORM   TURTLE

CICADA   INDIAN MEAL MOTH   HAIR BALL   TIME WARNER

WALK: IT'S TINY, DEAD, GOOD AT JOKES, GIVING YOU #

RUN: IT'S BIG, POISONOUS, CHASING YOU, LOOKS LIKE DAWSON

HIDE: IT'S SPITTING POISON, KEEPS SAYING "SUBTEXT"

4. DEAL WITH IT

TRAP IT
Make sure it's actually dead before lifting up the cup.

HAIRSPRAY IT
Grab the toxic shit & spray it 'til it lays still.

STOMP IT
Grab your docs, throw them as hard as you can.

HYPNOTIZE IT
Free your mind, the rest will follow (not recommended).

BREAKING THINGS

Whether or not you read Yeats doesn't really matter, but the man knew one thing for sure—things fall apart. They break, they fall off counters, they get stepped on. If you're clumsy, buy plastic & paper.

THINGS THAT BREAK EASILY

BOWLS

NAILS

INTERNET

PENCILS

HOW TO KNOW IF SOMETHING IS BROKEN:

WON'T TURN
ON

WON'T TURN
OFF

TURNS YOUR
ON TO OFF

HURTS
YOU

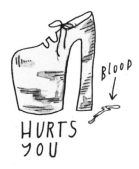

COME PREPARED

Nothing is worse than having the wrong tools, or worse, not having any. Get your butt to the hardware store:

STANDARD TOOLBOX

DUCT TAPE
SUPER GLUE
HAMMER
NEEDLES
THREAD
GATORADE
ADVIL

OTHER STUFF

RULER
PUTTY (SILLY OR NOT)
LEVEL
TINY SCREWDRIVER
TIME
6-PACK
TRASH CAN

LIST OF NUMBERS

ELECTRICIAN
PLUMBER
911
MOM
POISON CONTROL
(1-800-222-1222)

How to fix it:

PROBLEM	BOOKSHELF COLLAPSED	THE DOUGH WON'T RISE!	NETFLIX ISN'T WORKING
REACTION	READ BOOK YOU FORGOT ABOUT... (Too bad it's not a home improvement book)	CONSIDER MAKING A CRUSTLESS PIZZA (Hate self for even thinking it.)	OMG (WTF happens at the end of Buffy? Where is Spike?)
HELP!	GOOGLE IT	CALL MOM. THEN GOOGLE IT.	GOOGLE IS BROKEN!
FIX IT	REPLACE THE ONE MISSING SCREW....	BOTH WERE RIGHT! ADD MORE YEAST & ENJOY THE PIE!	GET DISTRACTED BY THE BROKEN SHELF. READ THE BOOK VERSION.

Fleischmann's RapidRise - Active - Yeast

Buffy

(When all is said & done, nothing lasts forever. If it's broke, fix it, flush it, or find a place for it. It takes some finesse to stashing your trash, so put some thought into where it goes.)

HOUSE-SITTING

House-sitting is both a delight & a burden. Chances are their place is nicer than yours & they have a higher sheet thread count, but remember, you can't cut the mustard if you spill it all over the quilt.

INDULGE

- Snacks
- Showers (& shampoo)
- Cable, aka Bravo Channel
- Trying on their clothes
- Couch naps
- Leaving notes from their pets

AVOID

- Having messy guests over
- Inviting pets over
- Pay-per-view
- Sleeping in their clothes
- Trying on their lipstick & then kissing every mirror
- Neighbors / law enforcement

DON'T WRITE A CHECK YOUR BODY CAN'T CASH
IN OTHER WORDS, HOUSE-SITTING HAS ITS CONSEQUENCES...

ONE DAY YOU AGREE TO HOUSE-SIT...

AND MAYBE YOU DECIDE TO GO OUT ONE NIGHT. (& YOU GO HARD)

AND MAYBE YOU BUY A SANDWICH ON THE WAY HOME...

OH HEY OV YEA

REALIZE SHOES ARE STILL ON, WHILE IN BED. FALL ASLEEP.

WAKE UP TO CAT PUKING ON BED & BRA. THERE IS SUCH A THING AS CAT KARMA.

HOME

WHAT YOU CONSIDER FREELANCE SOME MAY CONSIDER
UNEMPLOYED. OFTEN THE MOST IMPORTANT WORK
YOU CAN DO IS FAKING IT TIL YOU MAKE IT, WHICH
BEGINS WITH A "HOME OFFICE" & TIME WELL SPENT.

FROM THE DESK OF
Christie

Call it a studio, call it an office,
just call it something. You'll be
working here a while, so get
comfortable & get a name—you'll
need a place to have business
lunches delivered.

Ⓐ Ⓑ Ⓒ Ⓓ Ⓔ

OFFICE

Essentials

(A) SNACKS ON SNACKS ON SNACKS

(B) COFFEE, BOUGHT & HOMEMADE

(C) YOUR LAST CIGARETTE (GOOD, QUIT SMOKING)

(D) FANCY PENS FOR WRITING GOALS

(E) ATTEMPTED LIST OF GOALS

(F) MORE CAFFEINE

(G) READING MATERIAL

(H) COMPUTER (FOR RÉSUMÉ & RU PAUL)

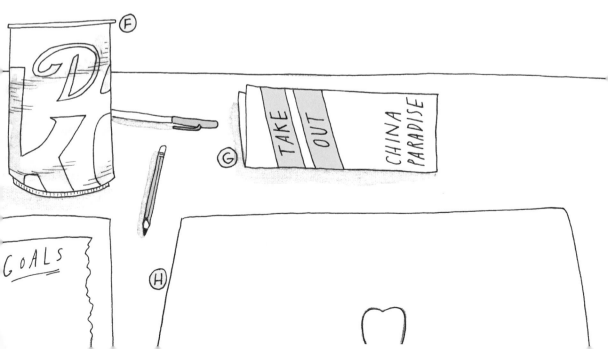

BILLS

Can you pay your telephone bills? Can you pay your automobile bills? If you can't, don't even think about chilling. There's nothing worse than debt hanging over you &, even worse, getting declined. Seen Troop Beverly Hills? Enough said.

WHEN YOU HAVE $

PAY ALL OF YOUR BILLS.

WHEN YOU DON'T HAVE $

DO WHAT IT TAKES TO PAY ALL OF YOUR BILLS...

ODD JOBS

SELL STUFF...

BAKE SALE!

EXTRA MONEY

Maybe you've won the lottery or a great aunt has died or you pawned some jewelry — either way, you've got money in the bank. And if the bills are paid (see: previous page), it's time to do yourself a favor & treat yourself. Student loans will always be there, that Acne dress on sale will not.

MONEY IN YOUR POCKET? LET IT BURN.

BUY A WIG!

INVEST IN GOLD!

monday

DIFFERENT SILK SHEETS FOR EACH DAY OF THE WEEK

GET A REAL DOLL & FOOL YOUR BOYFRIEND

LASER OFF YOUR TATTOOS & THEN GET THEM RE-DONE

CALL EVERY COUNTRY AT LEAST TWICE

Freelancing
WHEN "DAY OFF" MEANS EVERY DAY OFF

Monday

LOOK UP EVERYTHING ON THE INTERNET

Tuesday

PHOTOBOOTH YOUR FACE ONTO HOCUS POCUS MOVIE STILL(S)

Wednesday

PAINT NAILS 20 TIMES, NAME EACH LAYER, THEN SEE IF YOU CAN REMEMBER THEIR NAMES YOUNGEST TO OLDEST.

NAIL POL

Thursday

TWEEZE ENTIRE FACE

Friday

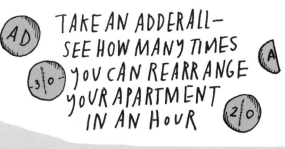

TAKE AN ADDERALL— SEE HOW MANY TIMES YOU CAN REARRANGE YOUR APARTMENT IN AN HOUR

AD 30 A D 20

the rest of the time...

PLAY 7 MINUTES IN HEAVEN ALONE, EMERGE FULLY SELF-REALIZED & IN A DIFFERENT SHIRT

BRUSH HAIR 1000 TIMES — EACH TIME SAY "BECAUSE YOU'RE WORTH IT"

SPA DAY! BIORÉ-STRIP YOUR ENTIRE BODY

PLAN

EAT CAN OF CASHEWS FOR BREAKFAST, Look UP GYMS FOR LUNCH

McC

LEAVE A SMOOTHIE OUT ON PORCH — COLLECT THE ANTS FOR ANT FARMS YOU CAN USE AS GIFTS FOR CHRISTMAS OR HANUKKAH

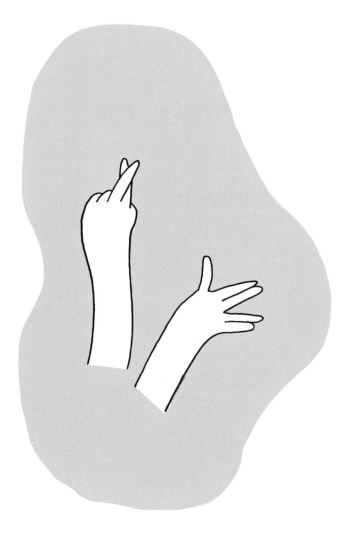

The body you have at 18 is not the body you'll have at 23 is not the body you'll have at 27. This will be a result of the combined efforts of sun exposure, drinking, eating, forgetting to eat, affordable haircuts, and permanent tattoos. You'll experiment with what you put on your body, then with what you put in your body, and then you'll figure out that your comfort zone lies somewhere in the oversized sweater & tortilla range. There's nothing to be afraid of when you're comfortable in your own skin, so sit back & relax, you're going to be there for a while.

Work With What You've Got

• BECAUSE IT'S ALL YOU'VE GOT •

REGAL NOSE

- LOOKS DISTINGUISHED
- SHOWCASES FRECKLES
- GREAT FOR SMELLING!

BUTT FOR DAYS

- LOOKS GOOD IN JEANS
- LOOKS GOOD IN THE NUDE
- GREAT FOR DANCING!

SO MUCH HAIR

- NEVER GO BALD
- NEVER GO COLD
- EXTRA PADDING ON YOUR PILLOW!

How to improve

TAMI TAYLOR

Look in the mirror & ask yourself "what would Tami Taylor do?" Then do it. Be proud of your gentle spirit & firm words. Blow-dry your hair, sleep in your makeup & know you look damn good when you speak your mind.

your body image

WHAT'S WORSE THAN NOT LOSING 5 POUNDS FAST?
NOT LOSING THE 5 POUNDS WHILE STARVING. WANT
TO LOOK BETTER NAKED? THEN FUCK FAD DIETS.
YOU LOOK BETTER WHEN YOU'RE HAPPY &
COUNTING THE CALORIES IN A TRISCUIT IS AS
FUN AS NOTHING. SO GO FOR A RUN OR RIDE
YOUR BIKE OR SWEAT TO THE OLDIES, JUST
DON'T SWEAT THE CREAM SAUCE OR THE
COOKIES. LOSE 10 POUNDS OR DON'T. SKINNY
IS ONLY SKIN DEEP & YOUR SKIN LOOKS GREAT.

IF YOU MUST...

DIET

- COLOR COORDINATE VEGETABLES TO OUTFITS
- ANY TIME YOU WANT TREATS SING "I WANT CANDY" INSTEAD (IT'LL ONLY HAPPEN ONCE)
- WHEN SODA CRAVINGS STRIKE, COLLECT A CAN FROM THE TRASH & REDEEM FOR MONEY!

EXERCISE

- ROLLER HOCKEY TO LOOK TOUGHER
- BEACH VOLLEYBALL TO LOOK TANNER
- YOGA TO LOOK EXTRA FLEXIBLE
- GOLF TO LOOK SWEATY (& RICH)
- MALL WALKING TO LOOK OLDER (MUCH OLDER)

. . . .

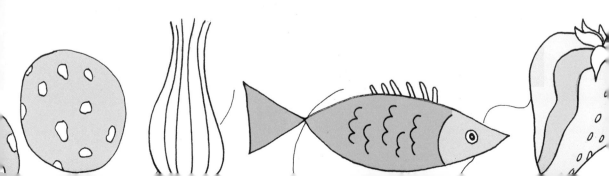

FEED YOURSELF

BASICS WHEN YOU'RE BROKE

—RICE $1 OFF —COUPONS   💧—WATER

—POTATOS   Honey —FREEBIES   —HOT SAUCE

WHAT YOU WANT, WHEN YOU WANT

The heart wants what the heart wants, and sometimes it's Doritos and sometimes it's a block of cheese in your underwear. Nothing is more boring than a woman who counts calories or doesn't know the value of Nutella and matzoh. Dig in— your mood depends on it.

CARROTS

CARROTS IN A BLANKET*

JUST THE BLANKET

| HERBIVORE | OMNIVORE | CARNIVORE |

*BLANKET IS BOLOGNA

SNACKING, SNACKED, SNAX

LIVE IT, LOVE IT

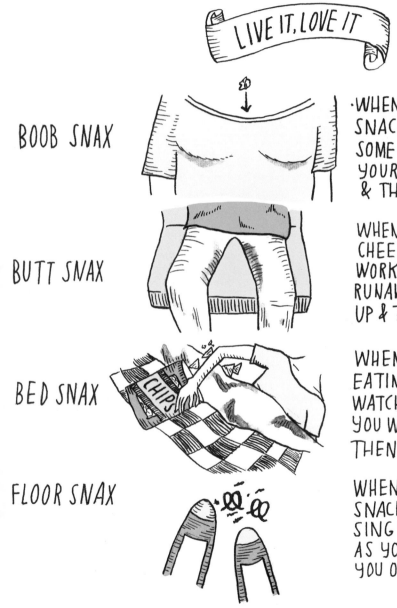

BOOB SNAX — ·WHEN YOU'RE STRAIGHT SNACKING AT YOUR DESK & SOME POPCORN FALLS DOWN YOUR SHIRT INTO YOUR BRA & THEN YOU EAT IT.

BUTT SNAX — WHEN YOU EAT A BAG OF CHEESE BALLS FOR LUNCH AT WORK & THEN FIND SOME RUNAWAYS WHEN YOU STAND UP & THEN YOU EAT THEM.

BED SNAX — WHEN YOU FALL ASLEEP EATING CHIPS IN BED WHILE WATCHING X-FILES & THEN YOU WAKE UP & FIND THEM & THEN YOU EAT THEM (STALE).

FLOOR SNAX — WHEN YOU DROP A NON-STICKY SNACK ON THE FLOOR & THEN SING "PUT IT IN YOUR MOUTH" AS YOU PICK IT UP & THEN YOU OBV. EAT IT.

SEE ALSO: BELLY BUTTON SNAX, HAIR SNAX, PURSE SNAX

Cheap Eats

BREAKFAST

- 2 BEEF STEAK TOMATOES
- 4 LARGE EGGS
- 2 TSPs CHIVES
- 1/4 CUP OF CHEDDAR
- SALT & PEPPER

Cut ≈1/2" off the tops of tomatoes. Scoop out guts & toss. Mix the other stuff together, & divide between tomatoes. Place in tray & bake at 350° for ≈45 minutes. Eat with toast.

LUNCH

2 1/4 cups BASMATI · A JALAPEÑO
13 oz COCONUT MILK · GARLIC CLOVE
1 CAN BLACK BEANS ·
1 MANGO, CUBED · CILANTRO

Cook rice with coconut milk— add water if needed. Heat beans. Mix everything else in a food processor. Put beans on top of rice & drizzle sauce on top. Add cilantro, salt to taste.

DINNER

Dissolve yeast in warm water. Add other ingredients & let sit for 10 minutes. Roll out on baking sheet, top with the toppings, bake @ 400° for ≈20 minutes.

- ONE PACKET OF YEAST
- 2 1/2 CUPS OF FLOUR
- 1 TSP HONEY
- 1 TSP SALT
- TOPPINGS

WORDS TO LIVE BY. CHEESE FOR LUNCH? BACON & BREAD FOR DINNER? YOU DO YOU.
FROM FOOD TO FASHION TO FRENCHING, DO IT IF IT DOES YOUR BODY RIGHT.
NEVER AN EXCUSE, BUT ALWAYS A REASON: BODY'S CHOICE.

YOUR BODY

SILK PANTS
NICE & SLINKY, BUT
BAD FOR BUTT JIGGLE.

NYLON DRESS
GOOD FOR CURVES,
DANGEROUS WHEN
WET (SWEATY).

TINY CUTOFFS
NEVER FORGET,
UNDERWEAR.

CROP TOPS
FOR THE CONFIDENT
AT HEART & THOSE
WITHOUT A/C.

SANDALS
MORE FUNCTION THAN
FORM—SO SPORTY!

FAKE NAILS
IF YOU'VE GOT
'EM, FLAUNT 'EM.

YOUR CLOSET

SERAPE
DOUBLES AS A BLANKET, GREAT FOR THE SHY.

FEDORA
GOOD FOR HALLOWEEN, MIAMI & GOODWILL.

HEADBANDS
ANYTHING THAT EMBODIES HILLARY IS A+.

LENNON GLASSES
FOR BEATLES & HARRY POTTER FANS ALIKE.

BROOCH
SENSIBLE, VAGUELY SENILE.

(SHEER)

SEXY SOCKS
DRAWS ATTENTION AWAY FROM EVERYTHING ELSE (SUCH AS YOUR BROOCH).

PERSONAL STYLE

Sometimes you dress, sometimes you dress for success &
sometimes you wear the same sweater 3 days in a row.
Regardless of a proclivity for short-shorts or scrunchies,
go bold or go home — there's no time to waste when it
comes to owning it (or borrowing it).

THINGS YOU NEED

Platform clogs

your Mom's jewelry

When you dream
about something &
then see it on sale

THINGS YOU CAN BORROW

Anything ugly-cute

Things that need
to be dry-cleaned

Something that
doesn't fit but it
looks so-so

THINGS TO PASS

Vintage that someone
has died in

Vintage with holes you'll
"fix later"

Shoes you get blisters from
when trying on

WEAR IT LIKE YOU MEAN IT:
NO SHAME = MORE GAME. WHAT YOU WANT, WHEN YOU WANT.

SHOES FOR SQUARE DANCING

(GREAT FOR INTERVIEWS)

BOLO TIE FOR DATE NIGHT

SILK ROBE AS PARTY DRESS

ACQUIRING

TRADING

WEAR THIS OK

"BORROWING"

FINDING

ORGANIZING

WINTER

SUMMER

SEASONS

("SEXY GOTH")

MOODS

(2002, FRINGE)

TRENDS

CLEANING

FEBREZE!

LEAVE OUTSIDE IN THE COLD

SPICED PUMPK

CARRY A SCENTED CANDLE

WHEN TO SAY

PIT STAINS BIG
ENOUGH TO LOOK
LIKE A BRA

YOU SEE A BABY
(OR ANIMAL)
IN THE SAME
THING

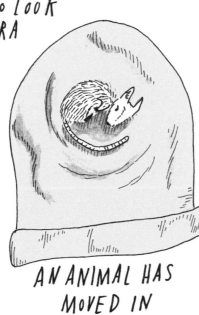

AN ANIMAL HAS
MOVED IN

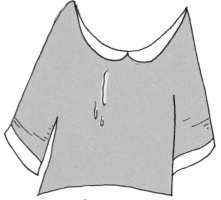

KETCHUP STAIN
RESEMBLES
BLOODY NOSE

CARING THE SKIN

THE BASICS

WASHING:
- Always wash off makeup!
- Exfoliate – use refined sugar on a wet washcloth & rub

MOISTURIZING:

KIEHL'S ULTRA FACIAL MOISTURIZER SPF30

- Make sure it has sunscreen!
- Oil-free for oily girls
- Try natural oils for dry skin: coconut, almond, or jojoba oil

PICKING:
- Don't do it (you will)
- Wash hands first, prepare for popping, wash face after

FOR YOU'RE IN

THE BREAKOUTS

THEY'RE BOUND TO HAPPEN, ESPECIALLY BEFORE INTERVIEWS, FIRST DATES & PERIODS (THANKS, BODY!)

- — Slightly red spot, cleanse as normal.

- — It's grown. What lies beneath? Pus. Pus & blood.

- — Pop! Now there's a hole in the middle. Fuck.

(You will pop it again while at work—it will bleed.)

- — Scab time. Cover-up won't help. Let it fall off on its own (unless you want scars!)

- —Put sunscreen on that spot! And everywhere!

AZTEC SECRET INDIAN HEALING CLAY

Like Bioré on steroids—this is all you need when all you need is every pore power-washed in 15 minutes.

AZTEC SECRET
INDIAN HEALING

Tattoo Time

From belly button rings to butt tattoos, how you mod your bod is gonna make a statement. Some are about who you are, some are about where you are & some are just about who you spend the most time with. Your tattoos will last a lifetime, haircuts will grow out in months & God help you with any holes.

WHY YOU DO WHAT YOU DO:

- ☐ WANTING TO PROVE YOUR UNIQUENESS
- ☐ TRYING TO PROVE YOUR REBELLIOUSNESS
- ☐ HOPING TO PROVE YOU'RE OVER IT
- ☐ 100% PROVING YOU'LL LIVE WITH IT
- ☐ SORT OF PROVING YOUR LOVE FOR IT
- ☐ BORED

NOTHING SAYS FOREVER
LIKE A NEEDLE HAMMERING
INK INTO YOUR BODY.
NO PAIN = NO GAIN.

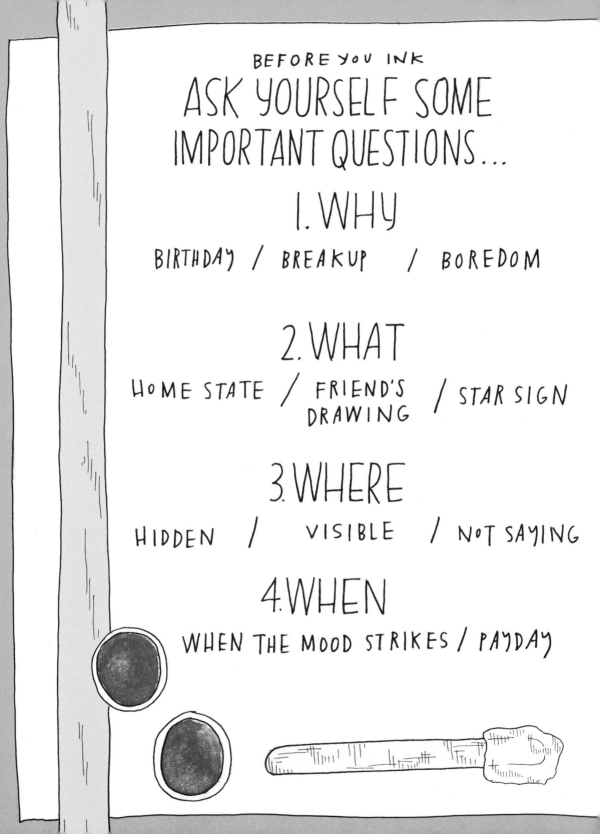

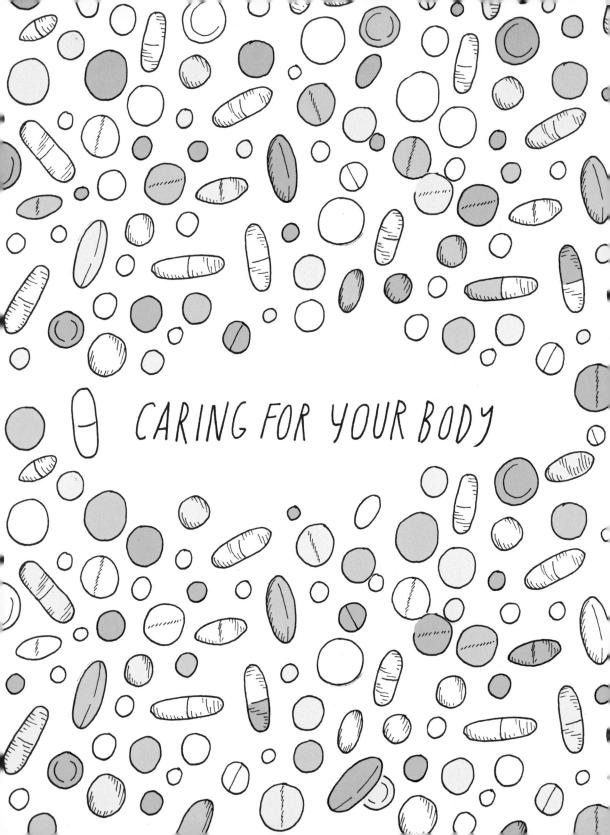

CARING FOR YOUR BODY

From pinkeye to pap smears, rarely does the time spent on WebMD make up for seeing a real MD. Sure, some things work themselves out, but that might mean losing all of your teeth in the process.*

GO REGULARLY
- OB-GYN
- DENTIST
- EYE DOCTOR

GO RANDOMLY
- DERMATOLOGIST
- GENERAL DOCTOR
- INTERNIST

GO RARELY
- ACUPUNCTURIST
- CARD READER
- ENERGY HEALER

GO HONESTLY
DON'T LIE ABOUT YOUR MEDICAL HISTORY! THEY CAN TEST YOUR BLOOD!

*Not really—this was just a dream I had when suffering from an untreated kidney infection.

GETTING SICK

If you've had the pleasure of getting shingles in the 8th grade, you'll know early on that life is full of injuries, rashes & unexpected UTI's. The more you know about your body the better the chances are it's either allergies or you're pregnant (same symptoms).

. . . . WHEN IT HAPPENS . . . .
On the road

HAVE SEX (AND THEN...)

DRIVE 9 HOURS OUT OF TOWN WITH MOM...

NEED TO PEE
try to pee
YOU CAN'T PEE

THE DESERT SHOWS NO MERCY FOR UTIs...

END UP IN URGENT CARE 3 DAYS LATER WITH A KIDNEY INFECTION

THE POINT IS—NEVER (EVER) IGNORE A UTI. SOME PAIN FADES, OTHER PAIN WILL REQUIRE A DRESSING CHANGE & NEW DEFINITION OF RIGHT-HANDED. YOU'RE NOT A DOCTOR (UNLESS YOU ARE), SO GO SEE ONE.

ARE YOU INJURED? FIGURE IT OUT.

WORST-CASE
true stories

WHEN YOU TELL YOUR EYE DOCTOR YOU'RE MOVING TO NEW YORK CITY & HE GETS A BIBLE OUT & READS ALOUD.

THE TIME YOU WENT TO YOUR YEARLY GYNO EXAM & THE DOC KEPT PAUSING TO TALK ABOUT TV.

THE NURSE WHO SAYS IT'S OKAY YOU CAN'T STOP PUKING BECAUSE "MAYBE YOU MIGHT LOSE SOME..."

THE DOCTOR WHO ASKS IF YOU'RE SEXUALLY ACTIVE (UH, YES) & THEN IF YOU'RE IN LOVE (UH, NO, YOU'RE 23 YEARS OLD).

BEST-CASE
possibilities

YOU THINK YOU'RE PREGNANT & YOU'RE NOT.

YOU THINK YOU'RE PREGNANT BUT YOU'VE
ACTUALLY LOST FIVE POUNDS.

YOU THINK YOU'RE PREGNANT & THEN THE DOCTOR
DIAGNOSES YOU AS HAVING A PILLOW IN YOUR SHIRT.

YOU DON'T THINK YOU'RE PREGNANT & THE DOCTOR
SAYS YOU'RE IN GREAT HEALTH.

If you were lucky enough to grow up with a mother who at times insisted that her real name was Bob & she was a man at some point but magically no longer, then I feel you. That grass always seems greener, other moms always seem more mom-like. But 15 years later you realize your family can be your friends & your friends can be your family & you really wish you could introduce Bob to your BFF because they would definitely get along. And as friends & families go, what you lack in one you can always make up for with the other.

REDEFINING FAMILY

YOU CAN'T CHOOSE YOUR FAMILY BUT YOU CAN CHOOSE WHAT YOU CALL THEM. AVOIDING TITLES HELPS YOU FORGET THAT YOU'RE RELATED ("JERRY" INSTEAD OF UNCLE), WHEREAS USING PET NAMES WITH NOT-BLOOD-RELATIVES CAN MAKE YOU FEEL EVEN CLOSER ("MY BABIES" INSTEAD OF CATS/TOMATO PLANTS/NOT BABY).

YOU

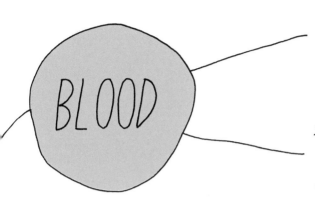

BLOOD

RELATIVES: EVEN IF YOU HARDLY LIKE THEM OR KNOW THEY EXIST.

ACCIDENTAL: INCLUDES ANY TRANSFUSION OR AGGRESSIVE FRENCHING WITH A NON-RELATIVE OBV) WHERE BLOOD IS DRAWN.

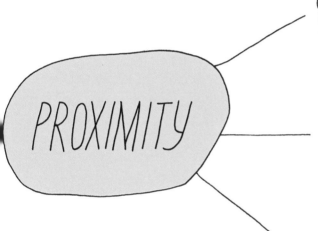

PROXIMITY

COWORKERS: THE PEOPLE WHO YOU ARE PAID TO SEE EVERY DAY (LOVE-HATE RELAYSH).

NEIGHBORS: SOME YOU SHARE A WALL WITH, OTHERS IT'S JUST THE BLOCK. REMEMBER— THEY MAY SELL CRACK BUT THEY'VE GOT YOUR BACK.

FRIENDS: BEST FRIENDS, TEXT FRIENDS, PARTY PALS, COFFEE FRIENDS, EVERYTHING IN BETWEEN.

OTHER

FRIENDS

BEST FRIEND

- LETS YOU BORROW ANYTHING
- LETS YOU TALK ABOUT ANYTHING
- TASKED WITH TELLING YOU WHAT YOU DON'T WANT TO HEAR

FORMER FRIEND

- DID SOMETHING SHITTY YOU WILL FOREVER REMEMBER
- STILL MAKES YOU ANGRY
- WILL BE REPLACED WITH BETTER PEOPLE IN THE FUTURE

SORRY, LATE

BE THERE IN 10

TWO SHAKES AWAY

WHERE ARE YOU

AN HOUR LATE

- HAS CAPACITY OF A NEWBORN TO TELL TIME
- NEVER SHORT ON EXCUSES OR TEXT MESSAGES

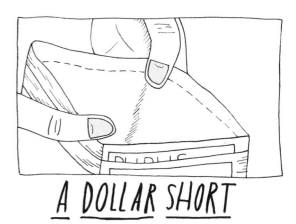

A DOLLAR SHORT

- WILL GIVE YOU MONEY TO BUY THEM A DRINK BUT NEGLECT THE DOLLAR TIP

FOREVER

SILENT PARTNER

- PAINFULLY SHY/QUIET/PMS-ING
- ALWAYS UNCOMFORTABLE AROUND YOUR OTHER FRIENDS
- LAST TO ARRIVE, FIRST TO LEAVE

THE FUNNY ONE

- GREAT ROAD TRIP PARTNER
- BAD IF YOU'RE A FREQUENT PEE-ER

SORRY, I'VE JUST BEEN **SO BUSY** LATELY! I WORKED ALL WEEK & HAD TO GO TO DINNER LAST NIGHT & YOGA THIS MORNING AND THEN

"I'M SO BUSY" FRIEND

- OMG SHE WORKS SO HARD
- YOU HANG OUT ON HER TERMS, FOR 30 MINUTES ONCE A MONTH

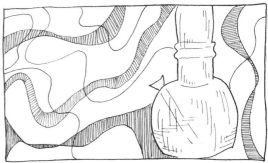

HIGH AND/OR MIGHTY

- DOUBLES AS LATE/HUNGRY FRIEND
- BELIEVES THAT THEY ARE THE FUNNY ONE RIGHT NOW.

Friends

WHAT TO DO WITH THEM

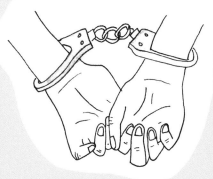

PLAY A ROUSING GAME OF "GUESS THE PERP" WHILE WATCHING ANY CRIME SHOW—ONLY FUN IF YOU BOTH LIKE HEINOUS CRIMES.

DURING THE SUMMER, PLAY A GAME OF "DIRT OR BRUISE"—ONLY RULE IS TO GUESS BEFORE YOU PRESS.

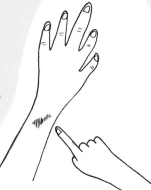

IN THE WINTER, PLAY "WATER OR ICE." ALWAYS PLAY WITH SOMEONE ELSE, NEVER PLAY WITH WITH THE PREGNANT OR OLD.

TAKE PHOTO-BOOTH COMPOSITE PHOTOS
THAT SHOW YOU WHAT YOUR
FUTURE KIDS WILL LOOK LIKE—
YOU TAKE IT FROM THERE.

COMPLIMENT EACH OTHER—NOT
ONLY DOES IT BOOST SELF-ESTEEM,
YOU GET TO SEE WHO THE BETTER
LIAR IS AT THE END OF IT.

You ARE LIKE So PRETTY & YOUR HAIR IS PERFECT.

PLAY "WOULD YOU RATHER" AND MAKE
"HANG OUT WITH ME" AN OPTION EVERY
TIME UNTIL THEY BREAK.

WOULD YOU RATHER
LICK A HOMELESS
GUY'S BUTT
—OR—
HANG OUT
WITH ME

Karaoke

REFUSING TO SING KARAOKE IS REFUSING TO BE ANY FUN. NO ONE WILL REMEMBER YOU FOR SINGING PAUL SIMON POORLY, BUT THEY WILL REMEMBER YOU TROTTING YOUR (BORING) HIGH-HORSE INTO A (NOT BORING) EVENING. YOU MIGHT MAKE SOME FRIENDS, YOU MIGHT MAKE EVEN MORE ENEMIES, JUST MAKE SOMETHING OF YOURSELF ON THAT MICROPHONE.

The Venue

PRIVATE ROOMS

MARIAH YOUR HEART OUT IN PRIVACY. IT'S ALWAYS MORE EXPENSIVE BUT AT LEAST YOU KNOW YOUR CROWD.

AT A BAR

YOU'LL NEVER SEE THESE PEOPLE AGAIN & LIQUID COURAGE RUNS DEEP. THAT SAID, THE BAR COMES WITH A FREE HANGOVER & PLENTY OF PLACES TO HIDE.

ON A STAGE

FOR THE TALENTED AND/OR THE FEARLESS. IF YOU'RE SCARED, DO A DUET — IF NOT, DO IT RIGHT.

Worst-Case
S C E N A R I O

YOU'RE VERY SOBER AND EVERYONE
IS VERY TONE DEAF.

THE ONLY THING AVAILABLE TO SING
IS ROCKAPELLA & PEOPLE ARE DOING IT.

PEOPLE ARE YELLING "KEEP YOUR DAY JOB"
& YOUR DAY JOB IS SINGING.

Best-Case

S C E N A R I O

YOU DON'T REMEMBER ANY OF IT &
NEITHER DOES ANYONE ELSE...

YOUR SONG CHOICE PUTS EVERYONE TO SLEEP,
GIVING YOU THE OPPORTUNITY TO CUT IN LINE
FOR THE BATHROOM AND/OR SNOOP AROUND.

THE CROWD THROWS DOLLARS INSTEAD OF FLOWERS
ON STAGE, MAKING YOU PAUSE TO QUESTION YOUR
PERFORMANCE BUT ALSO $30 WEALTHIER.

TRAVEL
with friends

THE TIME COMES IN A WOMAN'S LIFE WHEN SHE TRANSITIONS
FROM FAMILY TO FRIEND VACATIONS. SHE SWAPS BROTHERS
FOR BOYFRIENDS AND BEST FRIENDS AND COUSINS FOR
ANYTHING BUT. IT TAKES A SPECIAL SOMEONE TO HELP YOU
FLIRT WITH A SPECIAL ONE-EYED COWBOY, SO PICK YOUR
TRAVEL PARTNERS VERY, VERY CAREFULLY.

IT'S YOUR JOURNEY

NEED AN EXCUSE TO PACK UP & GO? THERE'S A REASON
TO FEEL EXTRAVAGANT IN ALL (4) SEASONS.

- Just graduated
- Just enrolled
- In search of healing

- "Needs to rest"
- Resting In Peace (endless journey)

- You're aging!
- Breakup trip
- You simply got lost

- Some kind of cleanse
- An excuse to get dirty

GET PACKING

EARPLUGS
In case your travel partner snores/you hate the sound of their voice.

TWEEZERS
For splinters/rogue hairs you don't notice until in public. Also to retrieve things you've dropped in airport toilets.

EYELINER
In the event that you're on a Cleopatra-themed cruise/you want to look older (draw wrinkles) or younger (draw freckles).

DECK OF CARDS
Make friends with magic tricks/alone time with solitare/play a game of strip poker as means of getting ready for bed.

BICYCLE PLAYING CARDS

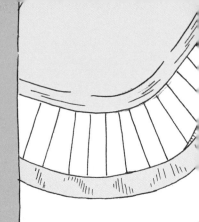

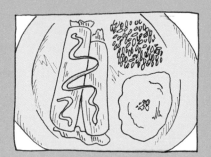

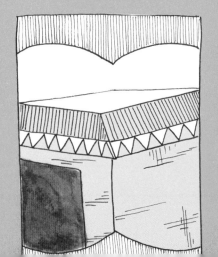

NUEVOS AMIGOS!

SOME FRIENDS MAKE GREAT TRAVEL PARTNERS, BUT NOT ALL OF THEM. IF YOUR SALTY COMPANION IS JUST TOO HOT TO HANDLE, TAKE A BREAK & FIND NEW FRIENDS.

· ·

NEW STRANGER-FRIENDS DO'S & DONT'S

DO...	DON'T...
EAT HOTEL BREAKFAST WITH THEM	TAKE CABS WITH THEM
PLAY GAMES WITH THEM	PLAY GAMES WITH HEARTS
EXCHANGE INFO	GIVE THEM TOO MUCH INFO
HANG OUT IN PUBLIC PLACES	FORGET TO INVITE YOUR FRIEND

NEW FRIENDS MAKE GOOD DINING PARTNERS, TOUR GUIDES & DATES.

YOU MAY ROLL YOUR EYES AT ROSES & ROBOCOP COSTUMES, BUT THERE'S SOMETHING TO BE SAID FOR THE HOLIDAY SPIRIT. NOW IS THE TIME FOR FORGING YOUR OWN FAMILY TRADITIONS, WHETHER IT'S WITH FRIENDS OR FLYING SOLO.

THANKSGIVING

When:
4TH THURSDAY OF NOVEMBER, YEARLY

the good:
IT'S AUTUMN / TOFURKEY IS ALLOWED

the bad:
YOUR FRIENDS AREN'T AS GOOD AT PRE-DINNER
SCRABBLE AS YOUR MOM.

Wear it:
SOMETHING STRETCHY THAT GOES FROM
DINNER TO BED IN ONE FELL SWOOP

Spare it:
ANYTHING HIGH-WAISTED (IT PUTS TOO MUCH
PRESSURE ON THE FOOD BABY)

Embrace it:
COOKING BEGETS A LONG DINNER BEGETS
HOURS & HOURS OF LOUNGING

CHRISTMAS

When :
DECEMBER 25TH

the good :
NO OBLIGATORY PRESENTS

the bad :
DEALING WITH ANYONE ON THE "SANTA-CON"
PUB CRAWL

Wear it :
SOMETHING THAT SCREAMS SEXY SANTA <u>OR</u> IS
VERY WARM BECAUSE IT'S COLD OUT

Spare it :
ANYTHING THAT REQUIRES BATTERIES AND/OR SHEDS

Embrace it :
YOU CAN'T ESCAPE IT & EVERYTHING SMELLS GOOD

HALLOWEEN

when:
OCTOBER 31ST

the good:
COSTUMES / CANDY / HOCUS POCUS ON TV

the bad:
FAKE BLOOD STAINS THE DAY AFTER

wear it:
SOMETHING ELABORATE, CONFUSING, SEXY, OR
NOTHING AT ALL (VERY SEXY)

spare it:
ANYTHING IMMOBILIZING

embrace it:
BECAUSE WHY NOT & MAYBE YOU'LL GET TO
MAKE OUT WITH AIR BUD* OR A GHOST

*THE ATHLETIC GOLDEN RETRIEVER

THE REST

When:
WHEN THE MOOD STRIKES & FEDERAL HOLIDAYS

the good:
GIVES YOU A REASON TO WEAR STARS & STRIPES OR MAX OUT A CREDIT CARD AT TARGET (DOLLAR AISLE)

the bad:
TRAFFIC & SNACKS GET PRICEY

Wear it:
APPROPRIATELY COLORED CROP TOP

Spare it:
THE WRONG COUNTRY'S COLORS/FLAG

Embrace it:
ONE DAY YOU'LL GROW OLD OR HAVE KIDS & NO LONGER HAVE THE TIME OR ENERGY TO CELEBRATE WITH FRIENDS. DO IT WHILE YOU STILL CAN.

SISTER

ALL IN THE FAMILY

YOU THINK YOUR FAMILY IS FUCKED UP?
SO DOES EVERYONE ELSE. AND WHILE
BLOOD IS THE TIE THAT BINDS, IT'S ONLY
AS STRONG AS YOU MAKE IT. FELON
COUSIN? SLEAZY UNCLE? GET IN LINE.

IN A PHASE

BROTHER

PENTECOSTAL AUNT

WORST-CASE
SCENARIO

YOUR FATHER WEARS A PAD <u>AS A BAND-AID</u> ON HIS FOOT WHILE ON A FAMILY VACATION IN D.C.

YOUR UNCLE SENDS YOU A TEXT MEANT FOR HIS (NOW) EX-GIRLFRIEND IN WHICH YOU LEARN ABOUT HIS SEX LIFE & POOR SPELLING.

YOUR GRANDMOTHER TELLS YOU THAT SHE HAD BIGGER BOOBS WHEN SHE WAS BORN THAN YOU HAVE NOW (34 B, THANKS).

MOM HAS A HABIT OF SENDING YOU TO SCHOOL WITH A PRISON-LUNCH OF JUST TWO PIECES OF WHITE BREAD, NO FILLING.

BEST-CASE
SCENARIO

YOUR MOTHER FINALLY STOPS ASKING WHY YOU
DON'T WEAR THE OVERALLS SHE BOUGHT
FOR YOU IN THE 5TH GRADE.

YOUR PARENTS REALIZE YOU DON'T NEED
A SHIRT FROM ANN TAYLOR LOFT AS
MUCH AS YOU NEED GROCERY MONEY.

NO ONE ASKS ABOUT YOUR LOVE LIFE,
SEX LIFE, WORK LIFE, PERSONAL LIFE, ETC.,
WHEN YOU DON'T WANT TO TALK ABOUT IT.

EVERY TIME YOU GO HOME, YOU ARE PICKED
UP FROM THE AIRPORT WITH A COLD
TOPO CHICO & A HOT BEAN & CHEESE TACO.

FOUR-LEGGED FAMILY

When two legs just won't do, you can always find a friend on all fours. It's the family you've always wanted & never had to explain yourself to. Be it fur or fins, it's your baby.

IS IT WORTH IT, LET ME WORK IT
(BECAUSE PETS ARE FUCKIN PRICEY)

LEAST $ — FISH — TURTLE — RABBIT — SEVERAL CATS — BEETHOVEN — MOST $

DOGS: Neediest of pets (what a dog wants, what a dog needs). Cost as much as a baby, but possibly more rewarding.

HOGS: Equivalent of non-prescription glasses— so very unnecessary.

RABBITS: The most protestant of pets, noisy as fuck & boy they smell.

CATS: Oh what a catpanion! Sometimes spells single & will eat you if you die alone at home (Ahhhh!).

ACQUIRING PETS:
there's a wrong way & a right way

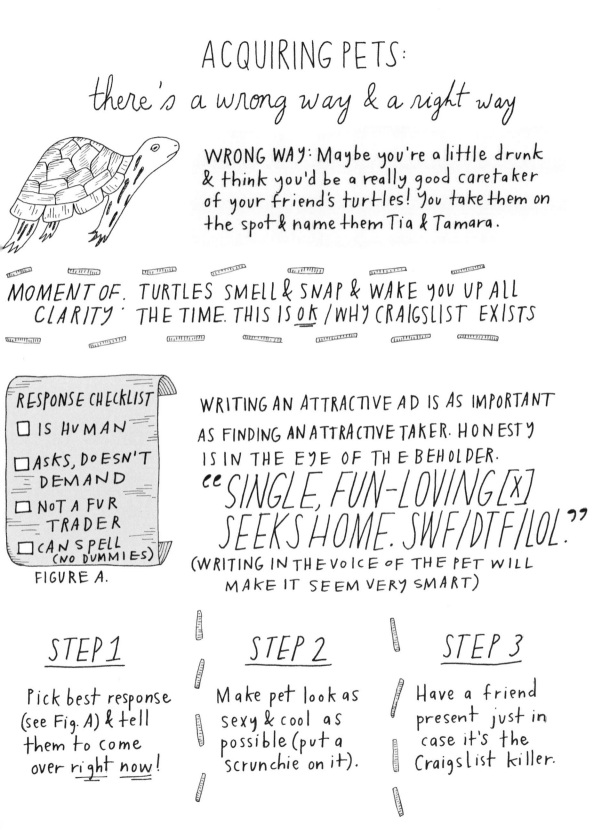

WRONG WAY: Maybe you're a little drunk & think you'd be a really good caretaker of your friend's turtles! You take them on the spot & name them Tia & Tamara.

MOMENT OF. TURTLES SMELL & SNAP & WAKE YOU UP ALL CLARITY · THE TIME. THIS IS <u>OK</u> / WHY CRAIGSLIST EXISTS

RESPONSE CHECKLIST
☐ IS HUMAN
☐ ASKS, DOESN'T DEMAND
☐ NOT A FUR TRADER
☐ CAN SPELL (NO DUMMIES)

FIGURE A.

WRITING AN ATTRACTIVE AD IS AS IMPORTANT AS FINDING AN ATTRACTIVE TAKER. HONESTY IS IN THE EYE OF THE BEHOLDER.
"SINGLE, FUN-LOVING [X] SEEKS HOME. SWF/DTF/LOL."
(WRITING IN THE VOICE OF THE PET WILL MAKE IT SEEM VERY SMART)

STEP 1
Pick best response (see Fig. A) & tell them to come over <u>right</u> <u>now</u>!

STEP 2
Make pet look as sexy & cool as possible (put a scrunchie on it).

STEP 3
Have a friend present just in case it's the Craigslist killer.

9 TO 5 FAMILY

COWORKERS ARE THE CURRENCY OF SANITY AND FOR RICHER OR POORER, YOU'RE STUCK WITH THEM 8-15 HOURS A DAY. YOU DON'T HAVE TO LOVE THEM BUT WHEN YOU BASICALLY LIVE WITH THEM, YOU NEED TO MAKE NICE.

THE SISTER

SCRATCHES YOUR BACK BOTH LITERALLY & FIGURATIVELY. SHE'LL GOSSIP & GET SALADS WITH YOU—A TRUE BEST BUD!

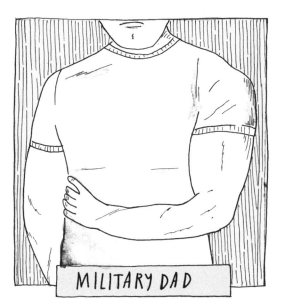

MILITARY DAD

A TIGHT TOP & BOOMING VOICE ARE HIS TWO BEST FRIENDS. NEVER SHORT ON SCARE TACTICS, HIS BARK IS BIGGER THAN HIS BITE.

BLOW HARD COUSIN

YOU HAVE NO IDEA HOW HE HAS A JOB AND HE MAKES $10K MORE THAN YOU. SHOWS HIS "PERSONALITY" IN AFFINITY FOR PING PONG & GRAPHIC TEES.

OLDER LESBIAN AUNT

WELL-CONNECTED & -INTENTIONED, SHE'S YOUR TOUGH-LOVE MOTHER HEN. DON'T GET TOO ATTACHED— SHE'LL LEAVE YOU FOR A BETTER JOB IN NO TIME FLAT.

THIS MISOGYNIST LOVES THE COUSIN, THEY ARE FRUIT OF THE SAME TREE.

PERVY UNCLE

A MAN WHO LOVES TO JUST "BUST YOUR BALLS"— HE'S KING OF THE BOY'S CLUB & DEFENSE MECHANISMS.

WEIRD DISTANT PERSON

WHO KNOWS WHO THEY ARE, BUT THEY KEEP SHOWING UP TO WORK. THEY WEAR SUNGLASSES INDOORS, SO ARE EITHER BLIND OR RICH.

love
line

Meeting, talking, sexing, dating, thinking you're dating, not dating but sexing, moving on, moving up, moving back, getting over it, getting over yourself, talking to yourself, talking to someone new, remembering there are so many someone-news, doing it again, you're doing it again. Make a promise to yourself that it won't happen again, ever again, until you meet a real stand-up guy.

PICK YOUR POISON:

THE UNEMPLOYED

- EXCESSIVE FREE TIME IS EQUALLY EXCITING & DISCONCERTING TO YOU

- CONSIDERS EVERY HOUR A HAPPY HOUR

- MILD DEPRESSION WRAPPED IN DIRTY CLOTHES, GENERALLY SLOW MOVING

THE OVEREMPLOYED

- MOMS LOVE HIM & HE LOVES BEING MOTHERED!

- CARES MORE ABOUT CLIMBING THE CORPORATE LADDER THAN CLIMBING YOU

- 14-HOUR WORKDAY LEAVES LITTLE TIME FOR FUN

Because everyone's got one

THE ARTIST

- IS HIS OWN BIGGEST FAN

- MIGHT BE WEARING YOUR CLOTHES, MOST DEFINITELY HAS A SPARE PAIR OF LEGGINGS YOU CAN BORROW

- COMMUNICATES MOSTLY IN TEXTS & ALWAYS ELLIPSES...

THE MYSTERY

- BACKPACK IS FULL OF EITHER DIAPERS, OR LOW-GRADE WEED

- LOOKS 35, COULD BE 53

- 100% HALF-GAY

MEET IN THE MIDDLE

Having trouble meeting people? Look around you — strangers are everywhere & they've all got potential. The guy on the train, the cashier at Chipotle, the dude with a dachshund — they're all options & they're all over.

Dry spell? Consider this:

- SOMETIMES OPPOSITES ATTRACT — LOOK FOR THE ANTI-YOU & SEE HOW IT GOES (TALL/ PIECES/ BLONDE).

- HANG OUT AT YOUR FAVORITE PLACES (DOG PARK, CANDY AISLE, ETC.) & YOU'LL FIND SOMEONE WITH AT LEAST ONE SHARED INTEREST.

- SPILL YOUR DRINK ON SOMEONE & WHEN YOU OFFER A NAPKIN TO THEM TO DRY OFF WITH, DON'T LET GO OF IT UNTIL YOU WHISPER YOUR NUMBER IN THEIR EAR & THEY CAN RECITE IT BACK TO YOU.

HOW TO FIND THEM:

Walking

- Bump into people, except for the blind because it's cruel.

- Walk very closely behind someone so that when they feel your breath on their back & turn around, you basically kiss!

- Circle them like a vulture so they know who the prey is.

Stalking

- Either learn their schedule or wait for them to get off work & ask where they're going.

- Look up everything you can online* & casually mention things you have in common (Burning Man, Aries, cousins).

Talking

- Say hello—a smile, a wink, a casual butt-bump will do.

- See if you like the sound of their voice / can imagine them saying your name in a sexy way.

- Too nervous? Imagine them nude, with a really gross body.

*IF YOU CAN'T FIND ANYTHING, CONSIDER THEM DANGEROUS (OR DEAD)

GET DIGITAL

NOT MEETING THE LOVES OF YOUR LIFE AT THE LANDROMAT? NO PROBLEMO — GET ONLINE. THERE'S NO SHAME IN HAVING DIGITAL GAME.

DATING SITES

They're not going anywhere & neither are you if you're a freak about it. You don't know until you try & sometimes it's worth trying over a cocktail.

FORUMS

You've already got weight-loss goals or a love for horses in common — covering the basics leaves more time for fun.

CRAIGSLIST

If animals are exchanged consider it an automatic relationship. It's the one place you can get a job, a couch, a free sack of size 10 socks & probably laid.

WARNING
- THE FREAKS: YOU'LL KNOW THEM BY THEIR PROFILE PHOTO OF ABS
- THE FAKE PHOTOS: ONLY HEAD SHOTS, LOTS OF HATS, WAIST-UP ONLY.
- THE FLAKES: THEY'LL MESSAGE YOU & MAKE PLANS & THEN DISAPPEAR

Are you into water sports?

I CAN'T TAKE YOU ON A DATE IF YOU DON'T LIKE OYSTERS.

BA

N REST IN AL TION?

ARE YOU OKAY? YOU LOOK LIKE YOU FELL OUT OF THE PRETTY TREE & HIT EVERY BRANCH ON THE WAY DOWN.

I can tell you're Jewish; can I take your picture?

COM OVE FO SON JAZ

I LIKE THE WAY YOU DECORATE YOUR SOUL

Can I take your shorts off with my teeth ?

OPEN RELAYSH?

YOU SHOULD BE A FASHION MODEL

let's get wet

SOMETIMES YOU MEET SOMEONE WHO
YOU COULD JUST TALK TO FOR HOURS,
AND YOU DO, AND THEN YOU WAKE UP
NEXT TO THEM AND REALIZE IT'S MORE
PANIC ROOM THAN **YOU'VE GOT MAIL** AND
DO THEY EVEN KNOW WHAT YOU DO FOR
A LIVING? IF YOU'RE EVER GOING TO FIGURE
OUT IF YOU LIKE-LIKE SOMEONE, TALK
TO THEM IN THE DAYLIGHT & SEE IF THEY
——————— TALK BACK. ———————

TALK the TALK

MENSA-MATERIAL IS ONE THING, SHIT FOR BRAINS IS ANOTHER. IQ AIN'T NOTHING BUT A NUMBER, BUT YOU NEED TO BE ABLE TO HAVE COGENT, IF NOT COHERENT, CONVERSATION WITH A PROSPECTIVE PARTNER. ALSO HELPFUL IN IDENTIFYING A LISP OR A SOPRANO.

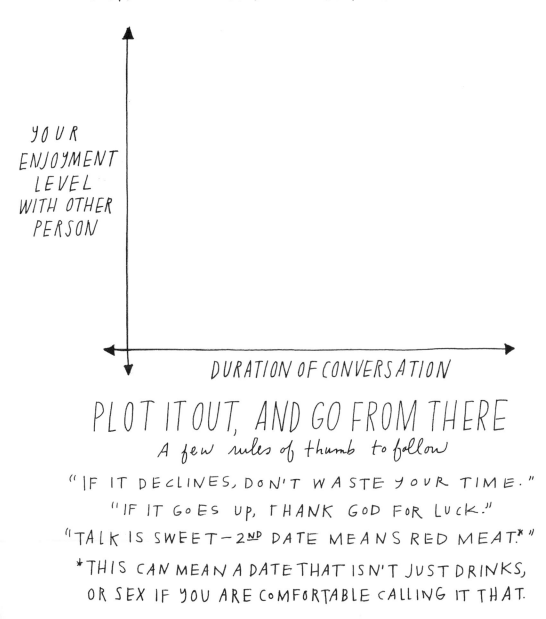

YOUR ENJOYMENT LEVEL WITH OTHER PERSON

DURATION OF CONVERSATION

PLOT IT OUT, AND GO FROM THERE
A few rules of thumb to follow

"IF IT DECLINES, DON'T WASTE YOUR TIME."

"IF IT GOES UP, THANK GOD FOR LUCK."

"TALK IS SWEET — 2ND DATE MEANS RED MEAT.*"

*THIS CAN MEAN A DATE THAT ISN'T JUST DRINKS, OR SEX IF YOU ARE COMFORTABLE CALLING IT THAT.

BUT WHAT DOES IT ALL MEAN?

EVERYONE SAYS THE BEGINNING IS THE BEST PART OF DATING THE TEXTING, THE NOT TEXTING, THE ASKING YOUR FRIENDS IF YOU SHOULD TEXT FIRST. SO FUN!!! BUT REALLY, WHAT DOES HE MEAN WHEN HE SAYS "TAKE CARE"?

> HOW WAS YOUR WEEKEND? TALK SOON!

All texts, no sex

Texts like there's no tomorrow or doesn't have a day job. It's fun & he's funny but so are your friends. It has the potential to get freaky, but more likely stays friendly.

All sex, no texts

Infrequent follow-ups after frequent "friendly hangouts." Where is he on a Friday night? You'll find out when he "sups" you on Sunday. Love it or leave it, because he's not changing.

> I'M BY YOUR PLACE — MIND IF I STOP BY IN A FEW?

The friendly follow-up

Mostly gone but never forgotten— you will hear from him as frequently as you forget him. The king of noncommittal, you like to think of it as nonconforming. What does he want? Your attention. Does it work? Just did.

It's been a while— how you doing?
—M

The emotionally (emoti-) conned

Words only serve as punctuation to their pictured vocabulary. This will forever betray his age & perceived maturity. The most confusing of the mediums, no one wants to figure out what sad pizza is supposed to mean.

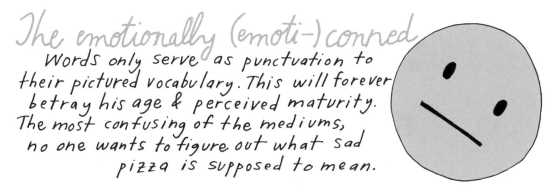

ARE YOU OVERTHINKING IT?

YES

MOST PEOPLE MEAN WHAT THEY SAY. TRUST YOUR GUT. IF YOU'RE STILL CONFUSED, ASK.

NO

THE MESSAGES ARE CRYPTIC & EVEN MORE SO ARE THE ACTIONS & YOU'RE ACTUALLY INVESTED IN IT.

EH

PROBABLY, BUT YOU HAVE THE TIME & YOU'RE CRUSHING SO HARD, SO WHO CARES? NOT YOU.

AND SO IT BEGINS
You're Dating
(OR ARE YOU? I'M NOT SURE, YOU MIGHT BE? TOO SOON TO ASK?)

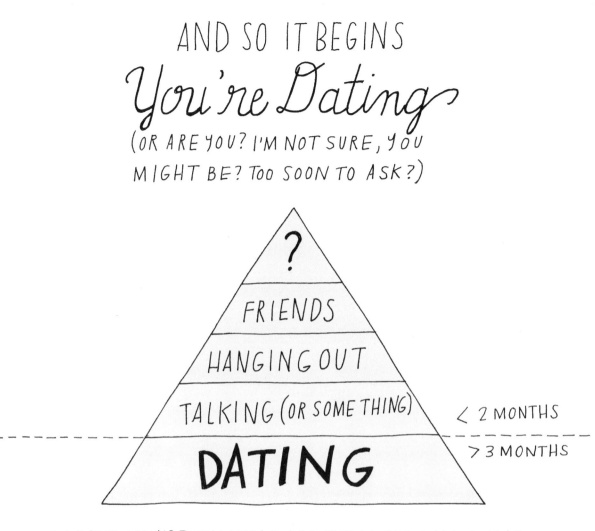

?

FRIENDS

HANGING OUT

TALKING (OR SOME THING)   < 2 MONTHS

DATING   > 3 MONTHS

MAYBE YOU'RE TALKING, MAYBE YOU'RE HANGING OUT. IT'S ALL SEMANTICS WHEN YOU'RE DOING IT TOGETHER. IF IT'S GOOD, RIDE IT – IF IT'S BAD GET OUT, AND IF IT'S NOT YOUR THING, NO BIG DEAL. AT TIMES IT WON'T BE HIS THING EITHER. MAKE SURE YOU'RE MORE PSYCHED THAN SICK OVER IT.

(GOOD) SEX ≠ DATING, DATING ≠ SEX.
YOU DO NOT HAVE TO BE DATING TO
HAVE SEX & YOU DO NOT HAVE TO HAVE
SEX TO BE DATING. THERE'S A WORLD
OF OPPORTUNITY IN THE PRUDE-TO-FREAK
SPECTRUM JUST WAITING FOR YOU TO
TIE IT UP & TALK BUTT PLUGS TO, SO
EMBRACE IT, WHATEVER IT IS YOU'RE INTO.

PRACTICE MAKES PERFECT

BECAUSE NO ONE GETS IT RIGHT ON THEIR FIRST TRY. OR SECOND OR THIRD. THE GOOD THING IS YOU CAN ALWAYS LEARN FROM YOUR MISTAKES.

A LADY IN THE STREET BUT A FREAK IN THE BED

A CERTAIN FRIEND ALWAYS COMPARES HER DUDES D-SIZES TO WHAT'S ON HER SPICE RACK; SOME ARE OVER-SIZED CINNAMON, OTHERS THE SMALL, THOUGH HARD-WORKING NUTMEG. AT THE END OF THE DAY THOUGH, THEY'RE ALL SPICES. SOME DAYS YOU'LL WANT SALT AND OTHER DAYS ALL-SPICE WILL DO. IT'S TRIAL & ERROR—SEASON TO TASTE.

THE OBVIOUS, FOR THE OBLIVIOUS

SAY WHAT YOU WANT

"PLEASE TOUCH MY BUTT, BUT HIT IT HARD & FAST."

AND WHAT YOU DON'T

"STOP SINGING THE NFL THEME SONG IN MY EAR DURING BONING."

TRY NEW THINGS

MAYBE IT'S SWAPPING OUT THE REGULAR CROTCH TOUCH (CT) FOR A BUTT TOUCH (BT), IN HEELS.

AND COME PREPARED

IF IT'S YOUR OWN HOUSE, HAVE YOUR OWN CONDOMS. YOU ARE NOT A CHILD, NOR DO YOU WANT ONE.

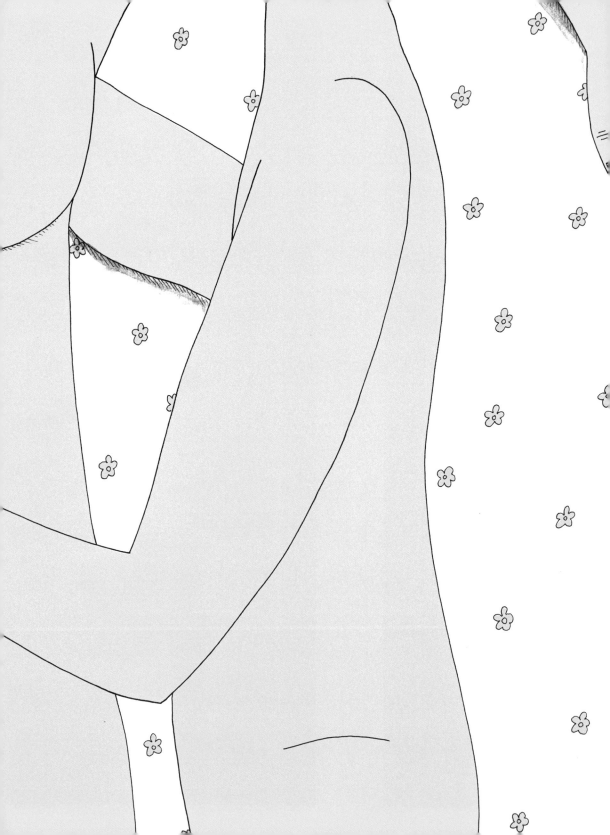

Consider Yourself
THREE TIMES A LADY

GO FOR IT

WHENEVER YOU WANT TO — THIS INCLUDES
TIMES WHEN LEGS ARE UNSHAVED, YOUR
PERIOD IS PRESENT, OR YOU'RE FEELING
FAT. IF THESE THINGS ARE IMPORTANT TO
SOMEONE, IT'S IMPORTANT NOT TO BONE THEM.

GO FOR IT AGAIN

IF THERE WAS TROUBLE GETTING IT DONE THE
FIRST TIME & YOU HAVE HOPE FOR THE SECOND
TIME. FOOL ME TWICE, SHAME ON ME.

NEVER AGAIN

IF YOU DON'T WANT TO, HE "DOESN'T FEEL
LIKE WEARING A CONDOM," DOESN'T GRASP
THE IDEA OF RECIPROCATION, HAS NO RESPECT
FOR YOUR SHEETS / BLANKETS / BATHROOM.

WORST-CASE
scenario

HE SPITS IN YOUR MOUTH EVERY
TIME HE KISSES YOU.

YOU FIND OUT AFTER DATING FOR
3 MONTHS YOU LOOK LIKE HIS SISTER.

A CAT PUKES ON THE BED WHILE YOU'RE
DOING IT TO SOMEONE & YOU DON'T REALIZE
IT UNTIL BOTH YOU & THE CAT FINISH.

YOU REALIZE YOU'VE LOST A TOE NAIL
AT SOME POINT IN THE NIGHT &
SOMEWHERE IN NOT YOUR BED.

BEST-CASE
scenario

YOU ORGASM 100% OF THE TIME.

AND THEN YOU HAVE BREAKFAST...

FOLLOWED BY NAPPING IN A COLD
ROOM THAT HAS A SURPLUS OF BLANKETS.

THEN REALIZING IT'S ONLY SATURDAY
& YOU GET TO DO IT ALL AGAIN TOMORROW.

AND NONE OF IT WAS ON AN
AIR MATTRESS.

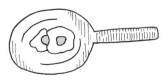

OVER IT

Breakups are the equivalent of summer sickness — they happen at the worst of times, you can never stop sweating, and as soon as it's over, it comes back for an encore. There's no prevention for a broken heart, but there's such a thing as coping.*

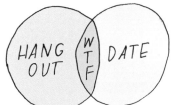

1. ENDURE "WTF" SPACE FOR 6-8 MONTHS.

2. OVER EMAIL, REALIZE HE IS TRYING TO "FIGURE THINGS OUT" RIGHT NOW.

3. PLAY WORST CASE SCENARIO — YOU HAVE DIED FROM LONELINESS & ARE A GHOST. THE NEW GF IS A BABE WITH A+ TEETH.

4. CONSULT PATTI SMITH. THEN TAROT CARDS. THEN THE CEILING ABOVE YOUR BED.

5. CONSIDER BANGS...

6. MAKE EYE CONTACT AT A PARTY. SMILE AT SOMEONE ELSE & LEAVE.

7. REPEAT 3-6 UNTIL YOU QUIT GAGGING WHEN YOU SEE HIM IN PUBLIC.

8. MEET A FRIEND OF A FRIEND AT A PARTY. CONSIDER YOURSELF MOVED ON.

*AND SOMETIMES IT'S NOT SO EASY

FROM BAD TO WORSE TO BETTER & BACK AGAIN.

- EAT EVERYTHING CONSIDERED A CHIP OR LIQUID; BINGE ON THE BIGGEST LOSER

- ONLY SHOWER TO REMOVE DORITO DUST

- QUIT EATING-DRINKING IN SHOWER IS OK

- BEGIN SHOWERING FOR RIGHT REASONS

- PUT ON REAL/CLEAN CLOTHES FOR 1ST TIME

- SWITCH TO SOLIDS & REMEMBER HYGEINE- CLOSE COMPUTER, CANCEL NETFLIX

AND FINALLY, THE BEST THING YOU CAN DO FOR YOURSELF IS TO REMEMBER ALL OF THEIR BAD QUALITIES & ALL OF YOUR GREAT ONES (YOU'RE PERFECT). SO CHEER UP & WRITE IT OUT — IT HELPS:

YOU
(All the good stuff)

EX
(Remember why it's over)

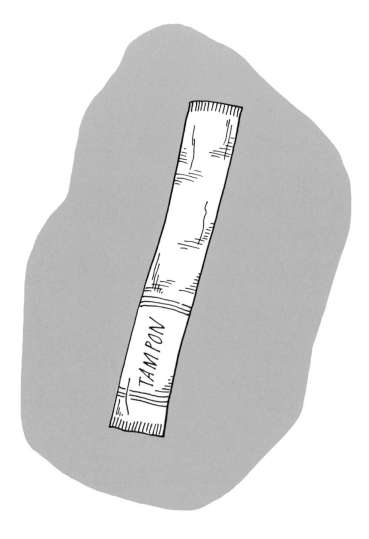

How many things will give me cancer? If he's a Cancer & I'm an Aries should I give up now? Do I trust Susan Miller too much? Do I trust myself not enough? How do I know if I can trust him? Every rational bone in that body has an equal if not greater unsettling thought waiting to sabotage it. You're okay. Or you will be okay.

GET YOUR FREAK ON:

SOMETHING BAD HAPPENING TO YOUR
NEW JOBS ONLY AT LADY FOOTLOCKER
HOW MESSY YOU REALLY ARE · THE IN
WEST NILE VIRUS · STOMACH ACHES AT
THIGHS! · DEADLINES · WHY THAT
YOU MAKING AN ACCIDENTAL JOKE
GLOBAL WARMING · CREDIT SCORE 300 · DOING YOU
YOUR CREDIT FOR [CREDIT SCORE 300] LIFE · STD.
ENOUGH · DID I TURN THE STOVE OFF?
CAN'T GET HARD · LIP/CHIN/NIP
WOMEN WHO DON'T SWEAT · PR
& SHOWERING · GENETICS ·
COMMITMENT · WASHING HANDS

TACO
512-4687

THINK YOU'RE ALONE WHEN IT COMES TO CRAZY?
YOU'RE NOT. FEW ADMIT IT, BUT WE ALL FEEL IT...

PET · LOSING YOUR JOB · FINDING
GHOSTS · · PEOPLE KNOWING
RNET & IT RUINING YOU ·
INOPPORTUNE TIMES · BUTT JIGGLE ·
DUDE STOPPED TEXTING · THE ODDS OF
ABOUT BLOWJOBS TO A CRUSH (100%) ·
TAXES WRONG & THUS FUCKING UP
THE FEDERAL BUDGET · NOT READING
· CANCER · · WHEN DUDES
HAIRS · THE WELL-DRESSED
NANCY · CHOOSING BETWEEN WORK
MOKING · THE GOP · BED BUGS ·
ENOUGH · MONEY — ALWAYS MONEY.

WORST-CASE
SCENARIO
(lies! they're all lies!)

YOU STUFF YOUR BRA EVEN THOUGH YOU
DON'T WEAR ONE 3/4 OF THE TIME.

BASED ON RESEMBLANCE, YOUR REAL
DAD IS WALTER MATTHAU.

SOMEWHERE ON YOUR BODY HIDES A
HOOTIE & THE BLOWFISH TATTOO.

YOUR REAL HANDS ARE THE SIZE OF A
BABY'S BUT YOU WEAR A SET OF PROSTHETICS.

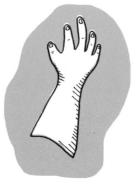

BEST-CASE
SCENARIO
(you'll take it!)

IT LOOKS LIKE YOU STUFF YOUR (34 B) BRA
BUT NO IT'S *ALL NATURAL!*

ALL OF YOUR JOKES ARE ORIGINAL MATERIAL.

YOU RUN AN 8-MINUTE MILE.

YOU'VE ALWAYS CHANGED YOUR OWN TIRES.

SALUTATORIAN!

YOU A BAD GIRL & YO' FRIENDS BAD TOO.

ALL YOUR NATURE FEARS, NATURALLY

INDULGE
- WHEN SOMETHING CAN EAT YOU RIGHT AWAY
- YOU COULD DROWN IN 60 SECONDS
- IT'S LIGHTNING OUTSIDE & YOU'RE SWIMMING
- FLESH IS CHANGING COLOR

AVOID
- THINKING ABOUT ANYTHING NOT SCIENCE-BASED
- SPACE-RELATED FEARS
- MOVIE-BASED FEARS
- FEARS BASED ON "FEELINGS"

EQUIVOCATE
EVERYTHING YOU DON'T UNDERSTAND
BUT STILL TRY TO EXPLAIN

FEAR OF BEING ALONE

PEOPLE FLAKE ON PLANS OR DON'T WANT GREEK FOOD OR JUST DON'T WANT TO HANG OUT, SORRY! YOU'LL NEVER BE AN INDEPENDENT WOMAN IF YOU CAN'T DO IT ON YOUR OWN.

SAY WHAT?! ⟶ FEELIN' WHAT? ⟶

EATING, ALONE

SELF-CONSCIOUS
SINGLE
HUNGRY

DRINKING, ALONE

SELF-CONSCIOUS
STRESSED
THIRSTY

CINEMARK 19
FRI. AUG 23 8:05PM
MAMMA MIA!
-RATED: PG-13
FRI 8:15P 08/23
=HOUSE: 9

THE MOVIES, ALONE

SELF-CONSCIOUS
SAD
BORED

→ DO WHAT? ————→ WHATEVER

BRING SOME-
THING TO
READ

YOU HAD A (GOOD/BAD/?)
MEAL & NOT A SOUL
CARED & NOW YOU'RE
DONE WITH IT.

THINK OF
SOMEONE
TO SEXT

BEN
BETH
BOBBY F.
BRIAN
BRIAN C.
CARRIE
CASEY
CAT

YOU'RE HAVING MORE
FUN BY THE END THAN
THE BEGINNING.
GREAT WORK!

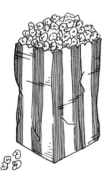

BUY SOME
SNACKS THAT
WILL SOP UP
ANY TEARS

DRY THOSE EYES & WIPE
THOSE CRUMBS OFF YOUR
CROTCH! GO FOR A WALK
WHILE DEBATING MERYL'S
BEST MOVIE (NOT THIS).

TREATS!

SHOWS

SHOPPING WITHOUT A 2ND OPINION ON ANYTHIN

WORKING

COFFEE DATE

MAREA

LIVIN LA VIDA *loner*

ONCE YOU BEGIN DOING STUFF ALONE YOU MAY NEVER STOP—WHICH ISN'T VERY GOOD FOR YOU BUT I GET IT.

TRY IT, SEE IF YOU LIKE IT, AND IF NOT, FIND SOME FRIENDS.

TRAVEL

PASSPORT

TATTOOS!

DANCING

ANY KIND OF SPA DAY

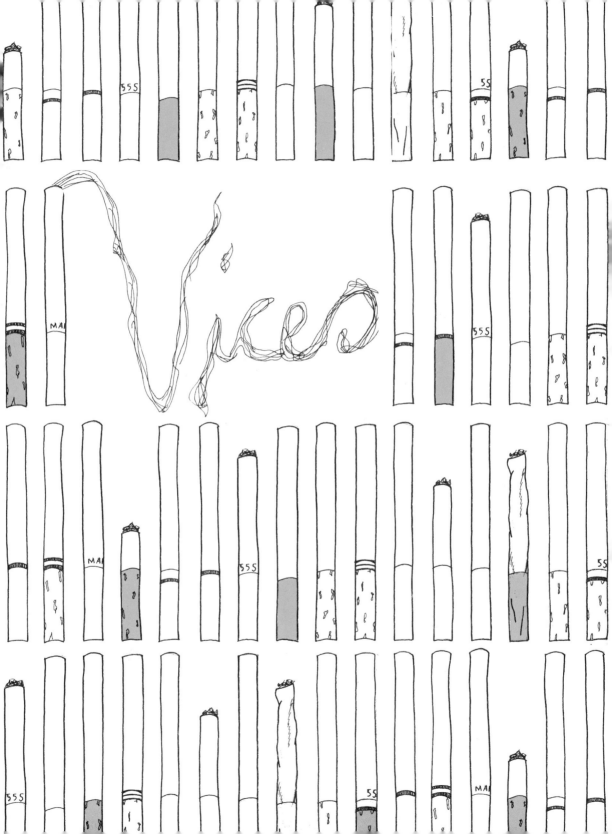

QUITIT

UNLESS YOU GROW UP WITH A BUTT-TON OF CONFIDENCE AND POSITIVE EATING HABITS, YOU'RE GOING TO END UP WRITING BUTT-TON OF CHECKS YOUR BODY CAN'T CASH. WHATEVER YOU'RE INTO, QUIT WHILE YOU'RE AHEAD.

1. IDENTIFY THE PROBLEM

 CIGS

 COFFEE

 SHOPPING

 BAD DUDES

2. DEFEND YOUR DEFENSE MECHANISMS

I only do it when I'm drunk or stressed!

IT'S PART OF MY CREATIVE PROCESS & OMG THESE DEADLINES

I NEED TO LOOK PROFESSIONAL FOR THIS INTERVIEW & THESE CROP TOPS ARE NEEDED

But he's so nice when he wants to be! ♡

555 FILTER KINGS

Strawberry Lip Smacker

3. FIND AN ALTERNATIVE

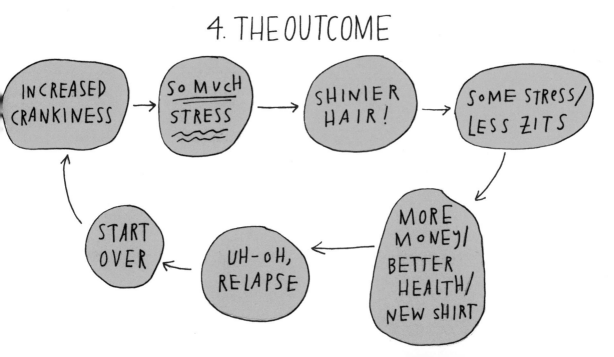

CARROTS   WATER   TRADING   NICE GUYS

Hi

4. THE OUTCOME

INCREASED CRANKINESS → SO MUCH STRESS → SHINIER HAIR! → SOME STRESS/ LESS ZITS

MORE MONEY/ BETTER HEALTH/ NEW SHIRT ← UH-OH, RELAPSE ← START OVER → (back to INCREASED CRANKINESS)

HANG

RULE OF THUMB:

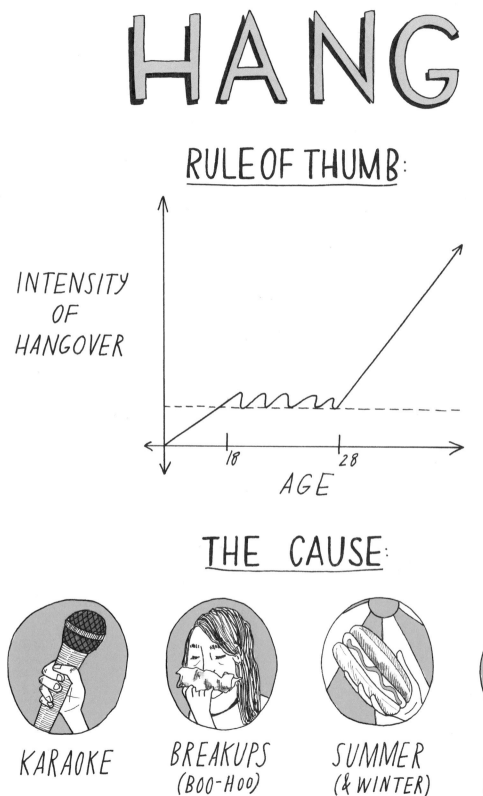

INTENSITY OF HANGOVER

18   28

AGE

THE CAUSE:

KARAOKE

BREAKUPS
(BOO-HOO)

SUMMER
(& WINTER)

ALCOHOL
(ALL OF IT)

OVERS

THE MISTAKE:

"ONE MORE & THEN I AM GOING STRAIGHT HOME."

"HA HA A NIGHT CAP DOES SOUND GOOD!"

"OH IT'S FREE?! OKAY!"

"LET'S GET CRAZY."

THE TYPES:

- SAD - YOU DRANK A 6-PACK OF DEPRESSANTS—NO SURPRISE
- SELF-CONSCIOUS - DID YOU "ACT SILLY"?! PROBABLY
- PAINFUL - EVERYTHING HURTS WHEN YOU RIDE THIS HORSE
- COMMUNAL - SLEEP IN BEST FRIEND'S BED; 2 TRU 2 B 4GOTTEN
- REGRETTABLE - WASTED $/WASTED TIME/WASTED

THE CONSEQUENCES:

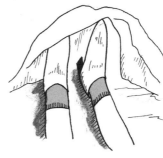

DRY MOUTH
SLEPT WITH MOUTH WIDE-OPEN & NOW TONGUE IS SANDPAPER.

SHOES ON
AND LIGHTS AND MAKEUP AND EVERYTHING.

CAKE IN A CUP

MARIACHI BAND

LOST EARRING

FLASHBACKS
YOU BUTTERFLY-EFFECT THE ENTIRE PREVIOUS NIGHT BEFORE.

HEADACHE
EVERY TIME YOUR EYES OPEN, A HAMMER GENTLY TAPS YOUR SKULL.

TRASH
APARTMENT LOOKS LIKE A FRAT HOUSE IF FRAT BOYS LOVED GATORADE.

BELLY PAINS
THE THOUGHT OF PUKING IS EQUALLY COMFORTING & PANIC INDUCING BECAUSE YOU HAVE THE LEGS OF A FAWN.

THE CURE:

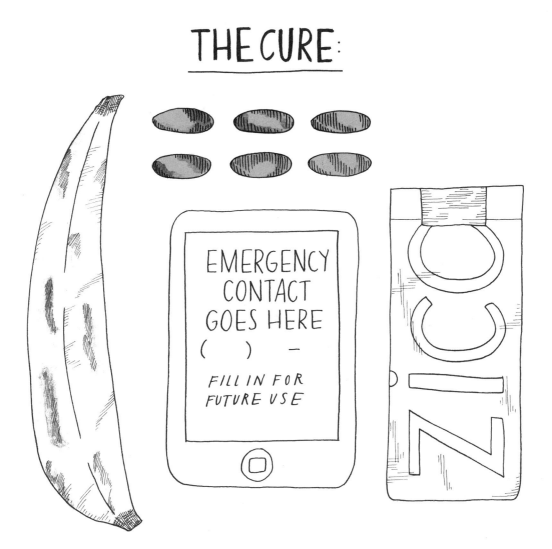

- BANANAS: CURES AS SOON AS SWALLOWED
- PAIN PILLS: OBVIOUSLY (BETTER WHEN TAKEN NIGHT BEFORE)
- PHONE: PRAY THAT IT'S CHARGED, KEEP NEARBY
- COCONUT WATER: SMELLS LIKE PUKE, KEEPS PUKE DOWN

I WILL NEVER DO THIS AGAIN, EVER. X_____

There's always more to talk about, but truth be told we're all a little tired & could probably use a shack & nap combo. Life is full of surprises (surprise!) and you're not always going to be prepared. Take solace in the fact that neither is anyone else. You may not be ready, but you've got this, girl.

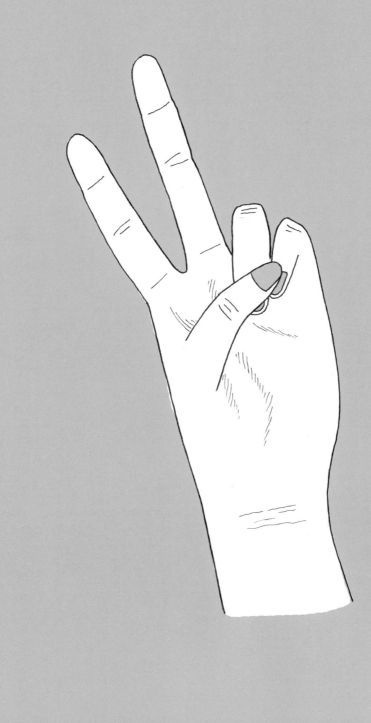

I WOULD LIKE TO THANK...
EVERYONE WHO SAW ME THROUGH
THIS BOOK: FAMILY, FRIENDS,
BEST FRIENDS, AND MY TEAM
AT POTTER STYLE & RANDOM HOUSE.
YOUR PATIENCE, KINDNESS,
PROOFREADING, CANDY, AND
SUPPORT HAVE BEEN SO VERY
MUCH APPRECIATED THROUGHOUT.
THANK YOU. —XTIE